C000220467

A Cumbrian Wildlife Garden

Richard Little

Illustrated by Christine Isherwood

BOOKCASE

Red Admiral and Small Tortoiseshell

Copyright: Estate of Richard Little
First edition, 2009
ISBN 9781904147473
Published by Bookcase
19 Castle Street, Carlisle, CA3 8SY
01228 544560; bookscumbria.com; bookcasecarlisle@aol.com

Printed and bound in Great Britain by
CPI Antony Rowe, Chippenham and Eastbourne

Introduction

The flame of interest in a hobby or pastime is usually initiated by several sparks. It is probably formed in early childhood and in fact may be a component of what we nostalgically call 'our earliest recollections'.

I can still vividly recall gazing in wonder at the tiny bright flowers of chickweed and sky-blue gems of eyebright. Through the eyes of a child, small and close to the ground, everything is new and fresh. Larger flowers such as gleaming yellow dandelions and the white lacy umbels of Queen Ann's Lace held a special fascination due to the presence of brightly-coloured flies and beetles. I remember being overwhelmed by the heavy sweet scent of May blossom along the lane near our house. This lane ran out onto a large area of commonland with flowery meadows, clumps of bushes and various ponds, enticing a small boy to explore unfettered and to learn about natural things. The commonland is still there but sadly the watery oases have long been filled in.

My interest in nature was also stimulated by the illustrations in books on pond-life and insects. I was particularly fascinated by colourful pictures of newts and giant water-beetles. It was a shock to find that the hideous monster in my jam-jar was the larva of the beautiful shiny beetle shown in the book.

About twenty years ago there developed a movement towards wildlife. After moving house to a plot with a somewhat bigger garden I decided to garden with wildlife in mind. In the local weekly paper there were several columns on gardening and a column on wildlife. I thought it was time to bring these two interests together in a single column on wildlife gardening. I started the articles seventeen years ago.

Recently it was suggested that the articles could be published as a book and I am grateful to *The Cumberland News* for their permission to compile them into book form. Thanks must also be given to Jeremy Roberts for his initial suggestion that a book could be of interest and for seeing the project through to completion, and to Christine Isherwood for the attractive drawings which complement the text so well.

All that is written took place within the confines of my garden. The problems were continuity and repetition. Radical pruning has been done. I hope the reader will enjoy these several journeys through a North Cumbrian wildlife garden.

Richard Little

September, 2009

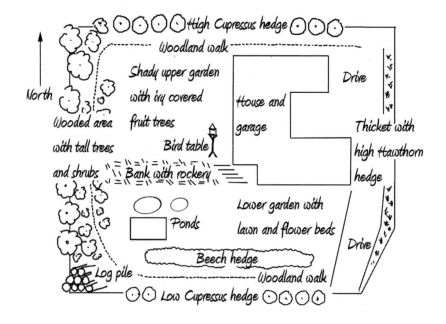

CONTENTS

2001   110

Jan.: hungry birds; *Feb.:* owl-box; *Mar.:* haughty pheasant; *Apr.:* delayed spawn; *May:* pot-bellied chicks; *Jun.:* the cragpie; *Jul.:* young goldfinches; *Aug.:* vole visitor; *Sep.:* three white butterflies; *Oct.:* take stock; *Nov.:* clean feeders; *Dec.:* two garden firsts.

2002   123

Jan.: tawny owl; *Feb.:* felonious field-mice; *Mar.:* tiny coal tits; *Apr.:* some moths; *May:* owl-pellets; *Jun.:* sparrow abundance; *Jul.:* woodpeckers; *Aug.:* adaptable corvids; *Sep.:* autumn-cleaning; *Oct.:* bold robin; *Nov.:* returning owl; *Dec.:* all change.

2005   137

Jan.: the great storm; *Feb.:* shrew – long-tailed tits; *Mar.:* starlings in an owl box; *Apr.:* newts; *May:* nest report; *Jun.:* may-bugs; *Jul.:* bank-voles; *Aug.:* unwelcome rat; *Sep.:* comma and chrysis; *Oct.:* redwings; *Nov.:* dawdling butterflies; *Dec.:* hazards of hibernation.

2006   152

Jan.: wary corvids; *Feb.:* countdown to spring; *Mar.:* buzzards; *Apr.:* first migrant; *May:* robin nests; *Jun.:* holly blue; *Jul.:* striking moths; *Aug.:* moth-trapping; *Sep.:* autumn rain; *Oct.:* late butterflies; *Nov.:* compost; *Dec.:* winter wagtail.

2007   167

Jan.: spring song in winter; *Feb.:* spring usher; *Mar.:* sparrowhawk; *Apr.:* frogless; *May:* magpies; *Jun.:* laggard tit youngster; *Jul.:* why no blue tits?; *Aug.:* fledgling wrens; *Sep.:* darter; *Oct.:* speckled wood; *Nov.:* horror-hop; *Dec.:* winter moths.

2008   184

Jan.: goldfinches; *Feb.:* bird-count; *Mar.:* herald of spring; *Apr.:* bathing sparrowhawk; *May:* goldfinch at last; *Jun.:* robin tribulations; *Jul.:* nesting news; *Aug.:* tree sparrow; *Sep.:* autumn moth finds; *Oct.:* planting for butterflies; *Nov.:* popular nyjer; *Dec.:* magic moments in the winter garden.

Author and Illustrator   201

Blue Tit

January

I know of several people in the Carlisle area who are modifying their gardens with the object of attracting a variety of animals, insects and birds around their homes and encouraging them to stay. I am sure there are many others who are also working to achieve this aim. For some time now I have felt that it would be worthwhile to have a monthly article for the reader with a leaning towards wildlife gardening. I hope over the coming months that I may interest such people with observations, suggestions and anecdotes concerned with wildlife gardening or simply wildlife in the garden.

I have no pretensions to being in any way an expert in gardening for wildlife, nor is my modest garden any different from many others in

Carlisle or the surrounding villages. I know several people who have adapted their gardens for specific creatures more successfully than I have.

Eight years ago I moved to my present house set in its one-third of an acre plot, situated a few miles outside Carlisle. The first action I took to develop my garden for wildlife was to plant some native trees such as silver birch, oak, and Scots pine, in a belt alongside the lawn to form a woodland edge attractive to birds. Trees such as oak also provide food and shelter for many species of insects and other invertebrates. I also made several small ponds in order to encourage amphibians such as frogs and newts to breed. Other modifications to the garden included planting buddleia, honeysuckle and other plants suitable for attracting butterflies and moths. I attempted, but not very successfully, to develop a mini-meadow of uncut grasses and wild flowers. Conventional gardening, with its emphasis on cultivated flowers, on tidiness and on killing things can create a hostile environment for insects, birds and wildlife in general. We do not have to turn our gardens into wildernesses, but we could reserve part of our garden for wildlife, a pond for frogs or a patch of nettles in a sunny corner for caterpillars of the Small Tortoiseshell butterfly.

January is a very quiet time in the garden. Most activity is centred on and around the bird-table. I have been watching three species of tit feeding on peanuts suspended from the table. The common little Blue Tits are bold and aggressive – even sometimes displacing the larger but more wary Great Tits from the nuts. The smallest member of the tit family, the timid and restless Coal Tit, quickly flies away on the approach of a Blue Tit. When I had a seed-feeder from which whole nuts could be removed, the Coal Tits rapidly removed all the nuts one by one, not to eat immediately but to store away. I now make them work for their supper by placing the nuts in a fine wire container. This gives the watcher more enjoyment and insight into their behaviour. Other birds which hang on the feeder are the stubby-billed Greenfinches and their similar but smaller relatives the increasingly common Siskins. Robins and Blackbirds feed on the scraps on the table, while the secretive thin-billed Dunnock or Hedge-sparrow picks up near-invisible crumbs on the ground beneath the table.

Two years ago, at this time of the year, a Hedgehog was hibernating in its nest of grass and leaves against the house wall. One afternoon, even though there was snow on the ground, I found it wandering around, presumably searching for food. Perhaps its store of body fat was running low. I fed it some scraps. This happened for two more days, and then it disappeared, perhaps to another nest. Whether it survived the winter I do not know. It was less than half-grown, about 400 grams. Hedgehogs have to reach a hibernation weight of at least 400 grams to survive the winter.

February

Tits and finches, including two pairs of Siskins, continue to visit the bird-table. A hen Pheasant regularly forages for food. Neighbours say this bird also visits their gardens on a regular basis. I have heard reports of Pheasants visiting gardens in adjoining villages for food and I wonder if this is an increasing occurrence.

A pair of Bullfinches regularly nips the buds off the apple trees. They announce their presence with a soft piping call. I have rarely seen a single bird, and never more than a pair together. Bullfinches may mate for life. Once a pair has formed a bond they do not seem to split up for the winter, unlike most small birds. I love to see these colourful visitors, but they can soon outstay their welcome, as they damage fruit-bearing buds.

One night during a period of hard frost I was awakened by a loud bark from under the bedroom window. A Fox had been attracted to the remains of a turkey carcass on the bird-table. It remained in the vicinity for about thirty seconds before moving off. I heard it on succeeding nights in the adjoining field and neighbours reported several sightings in broad daylight around the village.

Another visitor to the garden was a mole. I used to be amused by the seemingly neurotic reaction of people to the presence in their gardens of what I thought was a charming little mammal, until I had one! It first showed its presence with just two small hills. Each morning more appeared and on several occasions I saw the earth push up into yet another hill. However it became difficult to cut the grass and I was worried about damage to the plastic liner of my pond as the mole dug around it. I decided enough was enough and that it had out-stayed its welcome. I tried stamping on its tunnels, levelling the hills and spraying aerosols in its runs, all to no avail. I even borrowed a mole-trap, but did not use it. Fortunately both for the mole's well-being and my conscience it left before either was put in jeopardy.

A Sparrowhawk regularly visits the garden, its presence announced by the chorus of alarm notes from all the resident birds. I am always thrilled to see it as it dives over the hawthorn hedge, or sweeps through the Sitka spruce, sometimes clutching a small bird in its talons. I accepted it as a normal part of nature until one day in early spring some years ago. I had been trying to establish fantails in a dovecote in the garden. I obtained three pairs from a farm two miles away and kept them confined to the dovecote and an attached flight cage. This was to condition them to forget their previous home. I released them after they had been confined for four months, and to my relief they did not fly away but fluttered around the cote and fed from my hand. I very carefully withdrew to the house after about an hour, and then looked out of the window to watch them. To my horror a hen Sparrowhawk shot over the hedge and grabbed a bird, severely injuring it before I could scare it away. In fact when I brought the fantail into the house, the Sparrowhawk reappeared and started attacking the bloodied feathers left lying on the ground. The other doves had flown away, but the mate of the injured bird returned and fed it for several days while both incubated their eggs. It finally recovered, but still had a damaged wing. The other doves eventually returned.

March
A week ago, when cleaning out a kitchen cupboard, I disturbed a Small Tortoiseshell butterfly. This common reddish-orange insect often hibernates in or near man's habitation, such as in a loft, garage or garden shed. It can emerge very early in the year on mild days. It lays its eggs on the leaves of young nettles growing in a sunny position. I carefully placed the butterfly in a dark corner, hoping it would survive the remainder of the winter.

In my garden are several small ponds, two made with plastic sheeting, and the others rigid in design. Two contain fish. I am encouraging amphibians to breed in the others. There are five species of amphibians breeding in the Carlisle area. The Common Frog, Common Toad, and Common or Smooth Newt breed in ponds in, or close to, the city. The Palmate Newt, similar in size to the Smooth Newt, breeds further out in the countryside. The male Palmate has a thread-like extension to its tail and black webs on its rear feet. The much larger Great Crested, or Warty,

Newt, though a resident breeder, is more local and is protected by law.

I introduced newt tadpoles some years ago from sites that were being filled in for development. For several years I have seen Common Newts in the ponds, and what I thought were their tadpoles. Last year, when cleaning out one of the ponds, I placed some newts in a small tank for a week or so. I then noticed that eggs had been deposited on the leaves of Canadian waterweed in the tank. In a few days they had hatched into tiny fish-like tadpoles with external gills.

A mild spell at the end of January caused a movement of frogs in the swampy pond. However it was not until 19th February that the first lump of frogspawn appeared. When I made the first pond I introduced frog tadpoles from Penrith, which developed into froglets. Three years later a dozen frogs were breeding and each succeeding year up to sixty adult frogs were spawning in the ponds. I have also introduced toad-spawn into the ponds. Two years ago, one pair of toads bred. Last year two pairs bred. Toads are more difficult to establish than frogs, being more conservative in their choice of pond.

The spawning of the frogs had finished by mid-March but one day I found a female toad grasped by two male frogs, as if they wished to mate with her. I separated the misguided amphibians only to find half an hour later that I had to separate them again. Later, however, I heard the quiet piping of a male toad and found that, this time, it was he who had grasped the female. A few days later I found a male toad mounting a female frog. Whether this is a common event in the wild or part due in this case to the shortage of toads compared to frogs must be left to speculation.

April

A hen Blackbird is building in the Leyland cypress above the ponds. She is collecting dead grass from the flowerbeds to make her nest, but will not line it with mud, as does the Song Thrush. I have not seen much sign of Song Thrushes in the garden this winter, and it is only in the last few days that I have heard one singing. I began to think we were going to have a silent spring – at least as far as Song Thrushes were concerned. This thought took me back thirty years to when I first read the book *Silent Spring* by the biologist Rachel Carson. She was one of the first to warn the world that it was being poisoned by the mass use of herbicides and pesticides. They were getting into the food chains of animals, of people and particularly of birds, hence a 'silent spring'. Though governments have brought in controls and public opinion has changed, we can sometimes be thoughtless in the use of pesticides. Years ago I sprayed the gooseberry bushes for sawfly larvae and later found baby Blue Tits dead in their nest-box.

Several years ago I had two pairs of Song Thrushes nesting only sixteen metres apart. There were five broods in the season. Last year I had only one pair, which was unsuccessful. Our cat killed the hen, leaving two cold eggs in the nest. The cock sang continuously thereafter, for it had been denied its time-consuming duties of feeding its family and required a new mate. We had adopted our cat on a temporary basis as its previous owner had moved into a flat. It was a tom so we thought it would chase other cats away. We put a loud bell round its neck to warn birds of its approach. However it was both timid and swift. It allowed other cats in, and still managed to catch birds. Nesting birds were particularly vulnerable.

Each spring two pairs of Blue Tits and one pair of Great Tits nest in boxes in the garden. I hope each year that Coal Tits will nest. They prefer to nest in spruce trees. Again this spring a male is singing in the Sitka spruce. Another bird I hope will soon nest is the Goldcrest, the smallest British bird. A pair is currently resident and the male is singing. I hope they will build their frail hammock of a nest this spring.

May
Spring seemed to arrive in a rush one afternoon in late April. After a period of cool, wet and windy weather it became warm and sunny. Swallows dipped overhead, and the garden was full of the song of newly arrived Willow Warblers. These tiny greenish-brown birds migrate north from Africa in their millions, and their sweet descending song is evocative of summer.

A Collared Dove has built its nest, and its two eggs have hatched. I am amazed how small the nest is for the size of the bird! At first I thought the incubating bird was merely perching, most of its body being in full view from below. I was afraid that if the bird left its nest, which was whipping around in the rough wind, the eggs would be catapulted out.

Goldcrest

The Song Thrush has also finally built its nest, and a hen Blackbird is attempting to build only a few metres away from yet another nest containing young Blackbirds. Fights take place between the two hens but the males seem less concerned about the proximity of their nests.

Small Tortoiseshell butterflies appeared on 16th April, along with white-tailed bumblebees. They were searching the rockery for a suitable site, such as a vole hole, to start a new colony. Two Red Admiral butterflies were chasing each other on 30th April, an early record, considering the recent inclement weather. These beautiful scarlet and black insects may have migrated all the way from the Mediterranean, since they rarely survive the British winter.

I have left a patch of grass uncut this year to see which flowers will arise phoenix-like from the previously manicured lawn. Some flowering plants can survive unseen for years in a closely cut lawn, only to arise and blossom if allowed to grow. I have been rewarded with a beautiful flowering of lady's-smock, their lilac flowers covering the ground. This member of the cress family is the food plant of the orange-tip butterfly seen in the garden in May. Sadly one never again gets the full flush of flowering that one gets in the first summer after leaving the lawn uncut.

As yet I have seen no sign of House Martins over the garden. These neat black and white birds make their hemispherical nests under the eaves of houses. Many people are unhappy if House Martins choose to nest under the eaves because of the mess they make, but I was keen for them to nest when we first moved into the village. For two years no martins nested so I bought two artificial martin nests and placed them under the eaves. Still no Martins attempted to nest. Some time prior to another move to our present bungalow, I removed the artificial nests. Within twenty-four hours a flock of Martins circled and swooped around the house, twittering and clinging to the brickwork. After about two days all left, except for one pair, which stayed and started to build. I do not know if the young successfully fledged, as by that time I had moved. Often it is best to leave nature to her own devices.

June

In spite of the cold east wind and the night frosts that have plagued us in the latter half of May, the garden birds are having quite a successful breeding season. Two broods of Blue Tits and one of Great Tits are being fed by their parents, though at least one of the nestlings in each brood is undersized. One pair of Blackbirds are now rearing their second brood in the same nest, in spite of the fact that the cock was badly mauled by a neighbour's cat. I intervened in the nick of time!

Last year on 19th May I noticed a fleeting grey shape at the window. I was elated to realise that a Spotted Flycatcher had returned, soon to be joined by its mate. They flitted about the garden more like butterflies or bats than birds, returning to the same favoured perches that they had used the year before. The Spotted Flycatcher is the size of a Robin and predominantly mouse-grey in colour. It feeds on flying insects, caught in mid-air. Of our summer migrants it is the last to arrive, sometimes not being seen until the end of May. It is a creature of habit and will return year after year to a favourite nest-site. The nest is made of moss, wool and hair held together by cobwebs, placed in a cavity or creeper on a wall.

In early June two years ago, I noticed a pair taking an interest in the climbing-rose and trellis on the south wall of the bungalow. They built a tight little nest and laid four eggs, which hatched on 23rd June. I was very pleased that these birds were nesting, as they are an indication of a well-established garden. Twelve days after the eggs had hatched I noticed both parents were flying around the area but were not feeding their young. On investigation I found the young cold and sodden in the nest. Two days before, after a long dry period, we had had heavy rain, which had soaked and chilled the young. I was saddened to discover this and after some days saw no more of the parents. Last year the flycatchers made the same remarkable journey all the way from southern Africa to Europe, England, Cumbria, my village, my garden – and nested in exactly the same place as they did the previous year, laying five eggs. However tragedy struck a second time. When we returned after a few days away the eggs had gone, perhaps taken by the local Magpies.

All is not lost, however. A few days ago, on 28th May, the flycatchers arrived yet again, and are inspecting an open-fronted nest-box, the site of their previously abortive nesting attempts being occupied by House Sparrows. Third time lucky?

July

One pursuit the wildlife gardener can develop is an interest in moths, their identification and life histories. Butterflies may be more attractive, but there are only a dozen or so species to be found in a north Cumbrian garden. Several hundred species of moths may be caught in the same locality. The easiest method of attracting, capturing and so identifying these night-flying insects is by the use of lights. There are two common designs of commercially produced moth traps. One is the Robinson trap, which uses a powerful mercury vapour bulb. It is not very portable as it operates on mains voltage and so has to be run off a generator or from the mains. The other design is the Heath trap, which uses a much less powerful actinic tube powered by a twelve-volt motorcycle battery. It is less efficient than the Robinson trap but is much more portable. It can be used in remote locations and it only costs a fraction of the price. The principle of operation of both traps is that the lights attract the moths. They enter the body of the trap, which is designed to make entry easy but exiting difficult. The traps are filled with egg boxes under which the moths hide. Hopefully they are still there when the traps are opened after daybreak, when they are identified, recorded and finally released. The traps can be connected to a timer or a photoelectric cell so they only operate during the hours of darkness. As well as using both these models in the garden I have made a third trap from parts of both a Robinson and a Heath trap. I call this my Heath Robinson trap, which really is like the wacky machines invented by the comic artist of that name. In spite of its somewhat odd appearance it has caught more moths than the other traps. I hope more gardeners will take up 'mothing' as a hobby. When using a light as an attraction, it is surprising to see what is found in the moth-trap in the morning.

Recently a large heavy-bodied moth with beautiful rose pink wings was captured in the moth trap, an Elephant Hawkmoth. In late summer neighbours often contact me reporting sightings of little monsters looking like leathery legless lizards with big eyes, performing strange feats. These descriptions invariably refer to the full-grown caterpillar of the Elephant Hawk-moth. It is searching for a place to pupate after feeding on rosebay willowherb, *Fuchsia* or bogbean. The word elephant may refer to the trunk like extension of its front segments, which are extended when it is searching for food. When the creature is disturbed they retract and dilate to display false eyes that could deter an attacker. The whole caterpillar could be said to resemble an elephant's trunk. Next spring a beautiful stout-bodied pink-coloured moth will emerge from its pupa to produce more 'little monsters.'

Sometimes in the summer the security light comes on for no apparent reason. I have come to the conclusion that bats trigger the sensor, flying close in order to capture moths attracted by the light. Even though these bats slightly increase my electricity bill and reduce the moth population they are very welcome, adding interest to the wildlife garden. They are Pipistrelles, the commonest of our native bats. Two or three visit the garden at dusk.

A Hedgehog does its evening round. Last evening it was out in full light, crunching away at the slugs as they were beginning to emerge. The pair of Collared Doves has built another nest and a metre away from their first nest a Woodpigeon is sitting on two eggs.

Two metres up on the house wall I have a bird-table on which I place grain for the birds. To my surprise one morning I saw a Bank Vole scramble down the Virginia creeper from the roof with incredible agility. It ate some grain then descended to the ground. A humble wildlife garden can be an exotic place with pink Elephant Hawk-moths and acrobatic voles.

August

Perhaps the one thing that causes the wildlife gardener more frustration and heartache than anything else in the garden is the quality of the water in the garden pond. Ideally the water should be wine clear. As well as being aesthetically pleasing, clarity makes it easier to observe the many creatures that inhabit its depths. The ingredients for vigorous plant growth are sunlight, nutrients and water, as well as a warm environment. Nothing likes these conditions better than algae, particularly the unicellular variety that can turn pond water into a liquid resembling pea soup. The last few weeks of hot weather have provided the conditions for such a bloom. Tap water is nutrient-rich, as a result of run-off from fields dressed with chemical fertiliser. It is therefore better to use rainwater to fill the pond initially, and to top it up through the summer.

Oxygenating plants such as vigorous varieties of *Elodea* take up nutrients from the water and so long as excess growth is periodically removed, the chemical content of the water can be gradually reduced. Cutting down the amount of sunlight entering the water is also effective. This can be accomplished by allowing duckweed to spread over the water surface. The large floating leaves of water lilies reduce the amount of light entering the water. It has also been suggested that the use of straw can clear the water.

I remember as a boy in East Yorkshire cycling to a village pond several miles away to collect Daphnia, or water-fleas, with which to feed my tropical fish. These tiny crustaceans, related to shrimps, jerk up and down in the water – hence the name 'flea'. The source of this fish food was the village duck pond, complete with a large squadron of ducks whose waste indirectly fed the crustaceans, yet failed to cloud the crystal-clear water in which the swarm of pinkish Daphnia bounced. I wondered whether the presence of these creatures, feeding as they do on tiny organisms, was instrumental in keeping the water clear.

I recently resolved to test this hypothesis and obtained a stock of Daphnia, which I allowed to breed in a small pond in the shade of the wall. A few pellets of cat food were supplied as nutrient. After some weeks clouds of Daphnia appeared and I placed a considerable number in the other ponds. After a few days they had all disappeared. I replaced them every few days but each time they disappeared. They multiply successfully in the small pond but cannot sustain themselves in the bigger ponds. Whether they are quickly eaten or find the environmental conditions not to their liking I do not know.

September

On most days during the month of August a dozen or so Red Admiral butterflies avail themselves of the nectar secreted by the sweet smelling flowers of the buddleia. These mauve or purple-flowered bushes seem to attract butterflies from thin air. One may not see a single specimen of these insects over a wide area, yet the buddleia may be covered with several species.

The garden is now all but silent. The birds have stopped singing as the nesting season has ended. The screaming of the Swifts is no longer heard overhead. They left for the south during mid-August, one of the first of the summer visitors to leave, but House Martins and Swallows are still around. Some weeks ago a flock of these birds was swooping low in the garden after a cloud of flying ants. I had been puzzled at the appearance of particles of fine 'soil' on my window ledge. These were cleared away on several occasions but always reappeared. The mystery was solved one sultry afternoon when winged ants were observed emerging from fine cracks in the wood. There was an ants' nest in the wall below the window-frame and spoil from excavations had appeared from an exit inside the window frame. There are several nests of black garden ants, mostly under flagstones, in the garden. Winged adults emerge from all these nests simultaneously to take part in their mating flights during periods of hot, thundery weather.

Besides the resident Hedgehog and an occasional visiting mole,

Bank Vole

several species of small mammal make the garden their home. Of the two rodents, the Long-tailed Field-mouse is perhaps the commonest of British mammals. This mouse often enters my garage in the autumn to feast on the racks of stored apples. It is similar in size to the grey-coloured House Mouse but can be distinguished by its dark yellow-brown upper parts and pale belly. The other small rodent is the Bank Vole, similar in size but having a blunt oval-shaped head, small ears and a shorter tail. Two small insect-eating mammals also inhabit the garden; the small, restless Common Shrew, its pointed nose continuously searching for invertebrate prey, and its tiny relative the Pigmy Shrew, distinguished from young Common Shrews by its thicker tail. The bodies of these unfortunate animals are frequently found on the garden path, killed by the domestic cat.

October
The air is silent in the wildlife garden at this time of year, except for the plaintive autumn song of the Robin. Two pairs of Robins nest in the garden each spring and the rival males sing to each other to establish the boundaries of their territories. The areas of these should be sufficient to supply enough insects and worms to feed their hungry youngsters as well as themselves.

On the continent Robins are shy birds keeping to deep woodland, but in Britain they are bold enough to dog the footsteps of a gardener who might turn over a worm or two for them. I have even had one sit on a spade I was holding in my hand. Perhaps this is why the British section of the International Council for Bird Preservation chose the Robin to be Britain's national bird. The Robin is one of only a few species that are territorial in winter. The male and female birds hold separate plots and both sexes sing to advertise their territories, which are only half the size, on average, of the summer ones. The male and female divide the previous summer's territory between them, though former mates need not necessarily be neighbours.

During the last month, particularly after strong winds, there have been windfalls of apples. One has to be careful when picking these up, as underneath there could be several wasps. Common Wasps find ripe fruit particularly attractive in late summer. By this time they have finished raising their broods, and the workers spend the last few weeks of their lives gorging themselves. They can soon reduce an apple to a few pips and some pieces of skin.

In late spring, after hibernating, the queen wasp makes a nest the size of a golf ball from wood and saliva worked into a pulp. She then lays some eggs and when these hatch she feeds them with chewed-up flies. When the first workers emerge they take over all the work of the colony and extend the nest, until by August it may be the size of a football. This year in my garden golf-ball-sized nests were built in two tit nest-boxes. They were then abandoned – a football will not fit into a tit-box! From a human perspective wasps are beneficial during the summer months when they feed their young on insects, but are a nuisance at the 'back end' when they feed on garden fruit.

This is the season of the Michaelmas daisy and on sunny days they host numbers of Small Tortoiseshell butterflies, prior to hibernation. Another insect to be seen commonly of late is the Silver-Y, a large daylight flying brown moth. It is a migrant arriving in spring and producing a new generation in late summer when it becomes more numerous and conspicuous, hovering beside flowers as it feeds on the nectar.

The Swallows and House Martins have all but left, following the Swifts to Africa. A Willow Warbler is still sometimes seen, but all warblers will soon have left, save for an occasional Blackcap sustained through the winter by household scraps on the bird-table. The Starlings are flocking and each evening at dusk converging flocks pass over the garden heading for roosts within and to the east of Carlisle. We have passed the equinox and the dark days lie ahead. Soon the winter migrants will arrive from Scandinavia and the honking of geese will be heard as they fly over the garden.

November

The clocks have been put back an hour and the dark evenings have arrived, though during the day the autumnal colours of deciduous trees have been particularly vivid. The brilliant yellows, reds and oranges of birch, cherry and larch have been a delight to behold.

On the lawn several species of fungi have been observed, some grouped in characteristic circles or 'fairy rings'. Thousands of different kinds of fungi are found in Britain. They are most commonly observed in autumn when cooler, damper conditions may be more conducive to the formation of toadstools. These are the fruiting structure of the fungus, the main 'body' of the organism being a mass of threads below ground. Any reader who knows as little as I do about fungi, but would like to know more could not do better than attend a 'fungal foray' organised by a local Natural History Society.

In the tall hawthorn hedge, a dozen Long-tailed Tits are working their way through the branches, searching for tiny insects and spiders, lisping to each other with their quiet calls. A pair of Goldcrests, the smallest

21

British bird, accompanies them. House Sparrows are 'chewing' at the spent flowers of polygonum or Russian vine, also called 'mile-a-minute', due to the incredible speed at which it grows. This climbing shrub is ideal for quickly covering sheds and walls, providing shelter and nesting sites for birds in a season or two.

The hedges are covered in hips and haws, the fruits of the briar rose and hawthorn respectively. I can remember when rose hips were collected to make rosehip syrup, rich in vitamin C. Another berry of the field hedge is the sloe, the fruit of the Blackthorn. It looks like a tiny plum and it is thought to be an ancestor of the cultivated plum.

Our two winter-visiting thrushes have arrived, the Redwings and Fieldfares. Though a few pairs of both species may nest in Britain each year, the vast majority are visitors from northern Europe, particularly Scandinavia. The Redwing is like a small Song Thrush with a white eye-stripe and red patches under its wings. It has a thin high-pitched call-note, in contrast to the Fieldfare, which has a loud chattering call. This bird is similar to a Mistle Thrush but is easily identified by its blue-grey head and rump. These northern visitors add colour and movement to the wildlife garden during the dark winter months.

December

For several days recently, a dainty grey, black and yellow bird with a bobbing long tail has been doing the rounds of the garden ponds, picking off flies from the water's edge. It hops lightly from one lily pad to another to retrieve a drowned moth or beetle. This is the somewhat misnamed Grey Wagtail, the sprite of rushing mountain streams and moorland becks. It is a welcome, if unusual, sight in my wildlife garden, though in winter this beautiful bird may be found round lowland pools and sewage-farms. The more common wagtail visitor to my garden is the Pied Wagtail, which as its name infers is a black-and-white bird, also with a long bobbing tail. It nests in holes or cavities in banks or walls.

Autumn leaf-fall is a headache for the owner of a garden pond. I have tried covering the ponds with plastic sheeting, which is unsightly. I have also tried plastic netting, but small leaves such as birch and the needles of pine and larch slip through the mesh. One answer is to regularly sweep up newly fallen leaves floating on the water with a wide-meshed fishing-net like a child's shrimping-net, and to periodically dredge the decaying leaves from the bottom. The unsightly decaying leaves can make the water too acid, as well as reducing the oxygen content to the detriment of fish.

In pre-Christian times holly, ivy and mistletoe were considered special because they did not lose their leaves in the winter, as did other broadleaf trees. It was believed that holly berries warded off evil spirits. They are traditionally used as Christmas decorations. I have holly bushes in the garden, as well as ivy growing to about six metres up the high hawthorn hedge. I prefer to use plastic holly rather than destroy the shape of the holly bush by hacking off pieces of berried twig. The damaged bush takes a long time to recover, as holly is very slow growing. Ivy has a much more practical use in late autumn as its flowers produce copious quantities of nectar for moths and other insects when few other flowers are around. Its berries are much enjoyed by birds, especially Woodpigeons.

1995

Primrose

January

At the turn of the year the wildlife garden is not sleeping, but is in a cycle of continuous change. The winter jasmine has finished flowering, and the fragrant pinkish flowers of Winter-sweet have taken over. The green shoots of snowdrop, daffodil, crocus, and even the later-flowering bluebell push through the mat of dead leaves.

Naturalists have recently become interested in the increasing variety of bird species coming to bird-tables, particularly nut-feeders. As well as the usual tits and finches, a Dunnock has been hanging on the feeder in my garden, though it has not tried to peck out the nuts with its thin beak. I have heard of various devices to keep sparrows and Starlings off feeders.

The Greenfinches and Siskins have yet to appear in the garden this winter. Last year two pairs of Siskins stayed well into April and the males were singing as if trying to establish territories. I think it will not be long before they will be nesting in gardens.

February

The weather latterly has been particularly unsettled, periods of rain with strong winds alternating with gusty squalls of sleet and hail. In spite of these atrocious conditions a Kestrel has for the last few days been seen hovering over the grass in the field adjoining the garden. This small falcon, once known as the 'windhover', manages to remain stationary in relation to the ground by flying into the wind at the same speed as the wind is blowing it back. Many times I have observed it dive to the ground, on several occasions taking off with an item of prey in its talons, possibly a vole or mouse. I would be very happy if this attractive little raptor would occupy one of the two large nest-boxes I have placed in trees in my garden. I have made these boxes from drawers of a discarded chest. They are not the classic 'chimney-shaped' owl nest-box, but I wait optimistically for a Tawny Owl or a Kestrel to nest in them. I would also be pleased if other large hole-nesting birds such as Stock Doves or Jackdaws would occupy them.

I have a soft spot for Jackdaws dating back many years to when a friend gave us a nestling. He had been working on a roof and had no alternative but to remove the nest. We reared the nestling using a mixture of porridge, hard-boiled egg, bits of liver, and when possible, earthworms. We kept it in an outhouse for several weeks until it fledged and was released. Jack, as we now called him, would not fly away, but stayed around the house, flying onto our heads or shoulders whenever he saw us, completely imprinted on us. We fed him for some time, until eventually he appeared to be successfully foraging for himself. But he would still fly to us if we shouted 'Jack'. One day in late summer he did not come when called. We had seen the last of him.

As I look out of my window at the dismal winter scene, I notice the plumage of the male Chaffinches is developing a rosier hue. This is caused by the wearing-away of the dull tips of body-feathers grown in the autumn moult, revealing the brighter colours underneath in readiness for the breeding season. It is a welcome indicator of spring just over the horizon.

March

One of my favourite wild flowers is the humble lesser celandine. Its gold petals gleam against the rich green of its fleshy leaves. It is particularly welcome in early spring when there is little else to delight the eye amongst the drab still-dead vegetation. It brings back memories of early childhood, when I discovered these magical golden stars on the banks of a ditch on Beverley Westwood in East Yorkshire, where I grew up. I saw my first flowering celandine in a garden in Penrith on 4th February this year and a week later they were in bud in my garden.

When I trim the hedges or cut down perennials in the autumn, I stack the clippings in an elongated pile under the Sitka spruce at the bottom of the garden, making a habitat suitable for small mammals, amphibians and insects. On the damp ground in the partial shade were several clumps of celandine. I removed these clumps before piling up the rubbish. I placed the clumps around the ponds and in other damp areas of the garden. Each spring I am rewarded with patches of beautiful golden flowers.

The herbalists of bygone days believed in the 'Doctrine of Signatures', which postulated that plants indicate their medicinal value by the shape of their leaves, roots or fruits. Thus kidney-shaped leaves were a sure remedy for disorders of the kidneys. The bulbous roots of the celandine were thought to resemble haemorrhoids or piles, and therefore recommended as a cure for this unfortunate ailment, hence the alternative name for this member of the buttercup family, pilewort.

Once again this winter, the apple store in my garage has been visited by field mice. Only eating apples have been attacked, the mice scraping at the top of the fruit and excavating a concave depression surrounded by debris and droppings. Not one of the adjacent cooking-apples, Bramley Seedlings, was touched. Obviously field mice have a sweet tooth!

I heard a Mistle Thrush singing in early February. This bird sings from an exposed position, often in windy weather, hence its other name of 'Stormcock'. It is an extremely early nester, its nest often completely visible with no attempt at concealment. It is usually placed between a forked branch and a tree trunk, just as a small child would draw a bird's nest in a tree. The parent birds are very noisy and aggressive, even attacking cats that venture too close to their nest. The Mistle Thrush is larger than the more familiar Song Thrush, with brown spots instead of streaks on its breast. It also shows white flashes under the wings when it flies, rather than the orange flash of the smaller species.

Frogs appeared in the marshy pond on 12th February. I am amazed how varied they are both in colour and pattern; one female is bright orange. It would be interesting to see what colour its offspring would turn out to be.

April

Whenever April returns, I think of the wistful thoughts expressed in Robert Browning's poem *Home Thoughts from Abroad:* "Oh to be in England, now that April's there," which goes on to observe that *'the lowest boughs and the brushwood sheaf, Round the elm-tree bole are in tiny leaf'*. Browning must have been thinking of the south of England, or the climate must have changed since his day, because the elm hedge at the bottom of my garden is still stark and bare. Fortunately however, unlike most mature elms in the area, it has not succumbed to Dutch Elm Disease.

On 10th March I observed a pair of Long-tailed Tits hanging on the nuts. They stayed for some time, pecking busily, then flew away to return some minutes later. They repeated this performance several times over a period of about an hour. I was intrigued by their actions as normally I only see them pass through the garden as part of a mixed flock of tits. I hope they may stop to breed this spring, building their unmistakable oval-shaped domed nest, which, with its entrance hole near the top, has earned them their alternative name of 'bottle-tits'. The nest is composed of lichens, cobwebs and animal-hair, with a lining of up to 2000 feathers. A nearby chicken run is of help to them.

As I look out of my window I can see over a hundred frogs spawning. It appears as if the nearest pond is a solid mass of spawn. Frogs spawn in this pond first as it catches more sun and so is slightly warmer than the other ponds. The orange female I mentioned last month had two extra males clasped around its neck in addition to its mate. I managed to prize off these superfluous suitors, giving the female some relief, at least temporarily. Obviously orange is beautiful in the amphibian world!

A hen Blackbird is carrying dried grass into a holly bush and two pairs of Song Thrushes are squabbling over nesting sites. A male Dunnock with quivering wings is pursuing a female along the hedge, its usual nesting

27

site. A male Coal Tit is flying from tree to tree, marking out its territory by calling stridently and a diminutive Goldcrest is whispering its thin song in the Sitka. The nesting season has begun.

The arrival of spring can be compared to walking up a steep scree slope on a fell-side, two steps forward and one step back, and sometimes sliding back nearly to where one had started. So too with the weather, it progresses in fits and starts – one mild day then back to winter. Let us hope for a warm sunny spring – we never seem to get one now – and look forward to the summer visitors which should soon be arriving.

May

I saw my first Swallow over the garden on 14th April, after several days of warm spring weather. A Buzzard flew overhead, the first I have seen in our village, a couple of miles outside Carlisle. It was being mobbed by a Carrion Crow, one of a pair that has built a nest high up in an oak in the adjacent field. These birds have been visiting the garden to break twigs off a beech tree, a strenuous task! Why beech twigs in an oak tree?

A pair of Magpies is building their bulky nest in a Sitka spruce. The bottom of the nest is first lined with mud and completed with a layer of rootlets. The main feature however is the impenetrable dome of twigs, which protects the eggs from predation by crows or cats. I have an ambivalent attitude to the presence of these intelligent members of the crow family. I am excited at the prospect of another species of breeding bird in the wildlife garden, but aware of the Magpie's liking for the eggs and young of nesting songbirds. Only six metres away from the Magpie's nest, a pair of Woodpigeons is building a flat platform of twigs, on which will be laid two white eggs. These birds regularly feed on the fruits of ivy in the hawthorn hedge.

In spite of available secluded nesting areas, a pair of Song Thrushes has nested in an exposed position in a cedar adjacent to the drive, within a metre of passing cars. The nest contains four young. In my experience Song Thrushes nearly always build in evergreens, while Blackbirds' nests are more commonly found in deciduous hedges.

The sweet descending song of the tiny Willow Warbler fills the garden, while from the adjacent field comes the song of the Chiffchaff repetitively calling its name. Chiffchaffs usually prefer mature woodland but this individual seems to find a line of sycamores in a hedgerow a suitable environment. A constant rain of pieces of leaf advertised the presence of a pair of Bullfinches busily eating buds on the apple trees. I philosophically convince myself that fewer apples means larger ones. Beautiful twittering Goldfinches have been delicately removing the seeds from dandelion clocks, a good reason for allowing weeds to seed, though not always popular with neighbours!

The ponds are full of frog tadpoles feeding on the algal slime. Toads have spawned in the large pond I made two years ago. This is an interesting event, as the spawning adults were not reared as tadpoles in this pond. It is thought that toads are very conservative about their breeding pond, unlike frogs, returning to the pond they grew up in as tadpoles. Toads lay a double row of eggs embedded in a gelatinous string up to five metres in length. It is usually draped around waterweed. Common and Palmate Newts have also returned.

I will end with the solving of a mystery. I had changed from wire to plastic tit-feeders as the latter were easier to dismantle and therefore to clean. However, I recently found the nuts were disappearing at a prodigious rate. On examining the feeders I found that the plastic had been pecked through in various places, allowing the nuts to fall out or be easily removed. I marvelled at the efficiency of the tits' beaks until one day I saw a Long-tailed Field-mouse hanging acrobatically on the feeder. A half-grown mouse followed it, perhaps under instruction. It was not the beaks of birds but the teeth of rodents that had caused the damage. I have replaced the plastic feeders with wire ones. A friend who lives a few miles away tells me he has experienced the same problem with plastic feeders, but the culprits in his case were red squirrels.

June

As I write on 1st June, I reflect that this spring has been a curate's egg of a season, good in parts. Periods of hot weather reverted to wintry weather, with raw days and hard frosts at night, the bane of the gardener.

Squadrons of hoverflies have appeared on warm sunny days. They hang like tiny harrier jets above the spring flowers, their bodies mimicking bees and wasps. This gives them protection from prospective predators which fear their non-existent stings. One group of hoverflies, the droneflies, bear a close resemblance to honeybees. They were originally thought to be the subject of Samson's Biblical riddle *'Out of the eater came forth meat and out of the strong came forth sweetness'*. This quote is graphically illustrated on tins of a certain brand of golden syrup. The larvae of some species of dronefly feed on putrid meat, and it is now thought that the emergence from a rotting carcass of these flies is perhaps the basis of the riddle: the 'bees' were in fact hoverflies. The larva of one species of dronefly is called the rat-tailed maggot. Its pale slug-like body terminates in a long 'tail' through which it breathes, a necessity in the oxygen-starved environment of sewage or polluted drains in which it thrives. From our human perspective, the transformation of this revolting creature into a handsome active sun-loving insect is an actual recreation of the ugly duckling story.

I have been saddened to find the corpse of one of the pair of Magpies lying under its nest. On investigating I found that the six nestlings were dead, no doubt due to starvation. The other parent was still present, but spent its time anxiously calling for its mate, until after several days it left. It is possible that the local cat, which had been frequently mobbed by the birds when it approached their nest, caused its demise. The two young of the neighbouring nesting Woodpigeons have left their nest but have not yet fledged and are still being fed by their parents.

A Great Tit has eight nearly fledged young. This clutch size I have found to be fairly constant for the species, unlike the Blue Tit, which has a more variable, often larger, clutch size. A Blue Tit laid nine eggs. Eight hatched on 29th May, and the final egg a day later. This last chick is only half the size of its siblings. Will it survive? A Robin laid seven eggs, the largest number I have observed in the garden, though only six hatched. They are nearly fledged. Near my front door is a very small nest-box (9 x 7 x 15 cm), rather small even for the Blue Tits that have previously nested in it. But the entrance hole is 32 mm, large enough to allow a House Sparrow to lay four eggs in it. I was concerned how the nestlings of even this modest brood would manage in the constricted space. Two eggs failed to hatch and the remaining 'twins' have adequate space and are ready to fledge.

Large, Small and Green-veined White butterflies have been visiting the garden. The caterpillars of the first two feed on cabbages. The Large

White caterpillars are brightly coloured and gregarious, feeding on the outer leaves, while those of the Small White are green and live solitarily in the heart of the food plant. The only other butterflies I have seen this spring are Small Tortoiseshells and Orange-tips. It is interesting to note the number and variety of butterflies in our gardens and to encourage them by providing suitable flowers on which they can nectar.

July

I incorrectly estimated the bottom hedge in the garden to be at least a thousand years old. It is 30 m long and contains nine species of tree, and several species of woody climber such as bramble and wild rose. The formula for estimating the approximate age of a hedge is as follows. Mark the hedge into 30-stride lengths (about 30 m) and walk down each length counting all the woody plant species seen. Include the trees, but all woody climbers should be considered as one. You don't need to know their names: tell them apart by their leaves. Then calculate the average number of woody species per 30 m length, multiply by 100, and you should have the age of the hedge. My thousand-year estimate was invalid, as I used the number of relevant species from only one 30 m length of hedge. I am happy to have so many, mostly native, species of tree in the hedge.

Two weeks ago I had a walk around Wicken Fen, the National Trust nature reserve in the fenland of Cambridgeshire. In the reserve itself one has a feeling of wildness, but in fact it is an island, isolated in the prairie-like intensively cultivated biological desert of today's fens. In our area we are still fortunate to have a range of habitats, including mosses and unspoilt river valleys. Perhaps more importantly we have our gardens, in which the most natural constituent part is possibly the pond.

On the pond's surface whirligig beetles gyrate frenetically and long-legged pond-skaters chase after tiny insects trapped in the surface film. Rowing their way jerkily through the water with oar-like legs are the large carnivorous 'back-swimmers', *Notonecta* or water-boatmen. Their smaller more numerous cousins, the Corixids, are vegetarian. Hanging menacingly in mid-water, jaws at the ready, are the predatory larvae of various species of water beetle, the largest and most ferocious being the larva of the Great Diving Beetle. As a small boy I first came face-to-face with this fearsome creature when looking into a jam jar full of tadpoles, the contents of which it was happily devouring. At the bottom of the pond crawl the less aesthetically pleasing but equally interesting creepies: shrimps, pond-lice, larvae of flies, and the nymphs of damselflies and dragonflies.

August

Outside the nesting season, when they are silent, Song Thrushes can be very secretive, though their presence is advertised by little piles of snail-shells. As nearly every child knows, the thrush holds a snail by the lip of its shell and proceeds to smash the unfortunate mollusc against a stone or, as in my garden, the raised ridge of a paving slab, using it as an anvil. In my garden there are banded snails, but not the brown garden snails. Is this due to the lack of lime in the soil? When I first came to the Carlisle area I noticed some children used the word 'snail' to include slugs. This perhaps reflects a lack of familiarity with shelled molluscs. Their rarity is maybe a result of the type of soil.

The hot weather of the past month has caused a considerable loss of water by evaporation from the garden ponds. If the water is replaced by tap water an increase in salt content takes place. More minerals are added with the tap water but none are lost during evaporation. This can cause a growth in algae. Hopefully much of the mineral content will be absorbed by fast-growing waterweeds like *Elodea*, which, if frequently thinned out, can correct the increase in the mineral concentration. Ideally ponds should be topped-up using rainwater collected in water butts.

Pipistrelle Bats

At dusk up to four bats dive and twist over the lawn and along the edge of the trees, trawling for insects, including moths. They are most likely our commonest species, the Pipistrelle. As yet the flying ants have not taken to the air, though there has been feverish activity around the entrances to their nests during the hot humid weather.

The froglets and toadlets have left the ponds, the latter being smaller and darker with extremely thin legs – very insect-like. I have strimmed the 'mini-meadow', having waited for the spring flowers such as lady's smock, self-heal, bugle, cowslip and dandelion to set ripe seed. I raked off the cut grass to avoid enriching the soil, as over a period of years an increasingly impoverished soil will reduce coarse grass growth and so encourage meadow flowers.

Buddleias are now in bloom and have attracted considerable numbers of butterflies. They are mostly Small Tortoiseshells and Red Admirals. The former basks with its wings wide open, displaying bright reddish-orange upper sides. The adults hibernate, and in the spring lay their eggs on young clumps of nettles growing in warm sheltered positions. The adults produced in the summer behave in the same manner, but their offspring in August only feed in preparation for winter hibernation. The fast-flying Red Admirals, with their black, red and white coloration, are single-brooded. They are mostly migrants arriving in numbers from May onwards, some homebred adults adding to their numbers. The nettle is also the food plant of the Peacock Butterfly caterpillar. The numbers of this once common butterfly crashed in the mid-eighties, and have not yet recovered in the area.

September

The weather has been hot and dry for some weeks. It is unusual in Britain to wish for the sound of raindrops on our windows. It reminds me of when I lived in Central Africa where the dry season lasts for seven months. At least in Zambia the animals and plants had evolved to survive a prolonged drought. The dry season was a time of rest, just like our winter. In the second week of August the tall beech tree near the drive started to shed its leaves. They blew about the yard, dry and shrivelled, forming rustling piles as if it were October.

I tried to dig up worms for fishing, but nearly gave up as these soft-bodied creatures had burrowed deep and curled into knots to avoid desiccation, and only where I had watered were a meagre number found. Worm-eating birds like robins and blackbirds are faring the worst. They hop wearily across the bone-dry lawn, their prey well out of reach of probing beak, and listening ear. I have been providing them with moistened brown bread and have allowed them to strip the remaining currants and raspberries from the bushes. The paths are splashed with purple bird-droppings identifying the source of their food. Blackbirds are even attacking unripe apples. They normally eat them when they are ripe and soft.

Large numbers of moths have been caught in the moth-trap on these hot nights. One morning when I was in the conservatory preparing to release the specimens after identification, I became aware that a Willow Warbler was waiting outside the open window, ready to receive a free meal. When some moths escaped and settled on the inside of the window, the tiny warbler fluttered against the glass, pecking, in a futile attempt to catch the insects.

October
The month of October can have a melancholy feel. Some roses are still blooming in the garden, though the wild briar-rose is covered with hips. Several late-flowering perennials are in bloom, including several varieties of Michaelmas daisy beloved by late-flying butterflies. A dozen Red Admirals are at this moment feeding on these asters, a must for butterflies in the wildlife garden.

As I gaze out of my window, the skies are empty of House Martins and Swallows. They have followed the earlier-departing Swifts for southern climes, though flocks of Starlings have taken their place. Winter visitors such as the Redwings and Fieldfares have not yet arrived, though on 27th September when walking near Alston I saw a flock of the latter, after it had been sleeting! What a change from the hot dry weather of only a few weeks ago.

During the summer I have made wine from produce from my garden, starting with rhubarb, and followed by gooseberry, raspberry, and blackcurrant. There is no finesse in my 'bucket chemistry' approach to wine-making. A pressure cooker is used to extract the juice, but the result is quite palatable, or so I have been told! As mentioned previously I shared the fruit with the Blackbirds unable to reach earthworms because of the drought. Early-ripening soft-fleshed apples were nearly all eaten by desperately hungry and thirsty birds. A stalk and a piece of attached skin is all that remains of some fruit, still on the trees. Even the later ripening harder fleshed varieties have been attacked. The open wounds offer a place of entry for Red Admiral butterflies to sip the sweet juice. As well as the large numbers of Small Tortoiseshells and Red Admirals present this summer, rarer butterflies have been seen in the area, including the Camberwell Beauty, a large chocolate-brown insect with broad cream borders to its wings.

I was picking blackberries in early August nearly a month earlier than usual, a result of the excellent summer. The beech trees are heavy with beech mast and the oaks with acorns. The pair of Woodpigeons is feeding another pair of young. Autumn is a bountiful season for these large doves. Earthworms are again available to Blackbirds and thrushes, and a rash of worm casts has appeared on the lawn. The days are shortening and soon the leaves will fall, leaving a harvest of hips and haws for our resident birds and the winter migrants yet to arrive.

November

Today, 2nd November, it is mild, sunny and calm in the wildlife garden, the silence and tranquillity only broken by the sweet winter song of the Robin. The season of mellow fruitfulness is continuing into November after the mildest October in living memory. Red Admiral butterflies continue to visit the Michaelmas daisies along with the occasional White. My cupressus hedge is still growing. I sometimes think about limiting its height as it is beginning to cast too much shade. It is ironic that the gardener waits with enforced patience for years for hedges and trees to grow to their required height, and then worries about containing their growth.

The moth-trap has yielded a greater variety of specimens this October than usual, partly due to the lack of frost. I caught my first December Moth on 30th October, the date of capture belying its name. Earlier in the month I caught a Merveille du Jour moth, its appearance matching its exotic name, the beautiful green markings giving lie to the commonly

Grey Wagtail

held concept that all moths are boring and brown.

The hedges are covered with a red rash of rosehips and hawthorn berries and the holly berries are already ripe for the festive season to come. The slender twigs of elder are bent under their umbrellas of luscious fruits and I have never seen such an abundance of sloes, their sweet appearance belying their bitter taste. The local Crab apple trees have produced the heaviest crops I can remember. On the down side however, the apples I store over winter are quickly going bad, perhaps due to the damage caused to them during the summer by hungry birds, and also the current mild weather.

For some weeks now a Grey Wagtail, that 'sprite of mountain streams' has been visiting the ponds, on an almost daily basis. It prances across the lily-pads, catching surface insects such as pond-skaters and water-crickets.

There are other garden visitors with which I maintain an ambivalent relationship. A male Sparrowhawk seems to think that my feeding station of corn tray and peanut-feeders is for his benefit. It's not the bird food he wants, but the feeding birds themselves. Nearly every day he visits the garden and often flies at the feeders with their incumbent House Sparrows, even though they hang only ten centimetres from my living-room window. Usually all the birds escape into an adjoining tangle of Russian vine, but on at least two occasions the attack has been successful and he has flown off to pluck and consume his unfortunate victim.

Some weeks ago, on looking out of the window in the early morning, I saw a third visitor, a large grey Heron, standing beside the large pond. With horror I became aware of a large moving red shape in its bill: my largest and fattest goldfish, which seemed too wide in the girth for it to be swallowed. I banged on the window hoping the Heron would drop the unfortunate fish but it lifted its huge wings and flapped heavily upwards, carrying its burden over the Sitka spruce and away. A plastic heron stands guard by the pond, the assumption being that as Herons are loners when it comes to fishing, a passing bird would not land, mistaking the plastic look-a-like for the real thing. This assumption is flawed! I only have goldfish in this one pond, the other ponds being completely wild. So trying to be philosophical about the event, I conclude that the Heron is making certain that all my ponds are devoted solely to wildlife and not to exotic fish.

December

The poet Thomas Hood rather mournfully described the eleventh month of the year as having 'No shade, no shine, no butterflies, no bees, no fruits, no flowers, no leaves, no birds, – NOVEMBER!' Several of his observations have been invalidated this year. Many leaves remained on the trees well into November and I cannot remember ever having seen such a glorious autumn, the oak trees being particularly splendid. There has been a bountiful harvest of berries and the garden flowers continued to bloom up to the end of the month, including honeysuckle and dandelions. On 26th November during an interval of subdued sunshine a Small Tortoiseshell butterfly flitted over the trees.

Fallen leaves have been blown into the ponds. As well as being unsightly, decaying leaves can cause pollution and a lowering of the oxygen content of the water, to the detriment of aquatic life. The water in the large pond is now clear, possibly due in part to bundles of straw that were weighed down to the bottom earlier in the year. I have not seen any remaining goldfish in this pond; the visiting Heron appears to have taken them all.

I recently found a somewhat dehydrated newt on the kitchen floor. It was a female Smooth (or Common) Newt and how it got in to the house is a mystery, as there is no direct outside access. There must be a ventilator or gap that I do not know of. It is particularly strange as the same thing happened last winter. I placed the shrunken amphibian in a bowl of water and it slowly swelled to its usual size. I then released it into a secluded part of the rockery where I hope its peers, along with the garden toads, were already hibernating.

The height of my west-facing cupressus hedge has been lowered by three metres as it was increasingly shading the ponds and inhibiting the growth of the water plants. In the tangle of fallen branches lay the remains of the Woodpigeons' nest. It was interesting to note that it was in three layers. Presumably the birds built one on top of another, laying another clutch in a new nest after the previous brood had fledged.

Dog-rose; bramble

January

The three common species of tit regularly visit the feeders; the Great Tit with its black head, the smaller Blue Tit and the equally small Coal Tit, also black headed but with a white flash. It is imperative during severe weather that the birds have access to water. A saucerful soon freezes over, so it should be refilled frequently with tepid water.

I often catch sight of a tiny shape flitting from the nest-box at the front door. Several Wrens are roosting there, snug in their dry and draught-free refuge. By packing together in sub-zero weather they reduce their surface area-to-weight ratio and so slow down heat loss.

Recently I noticed two mouse-like birds spiralling up the trunk of an apple tree, their fine curved beaks probing for spiders and hibernating

Redpoll

insects. These Robin-sized birds, brown above and silvery-white beneath, are aptly named Tree Creepers. They usually nest behind loose bark or other tree cavities. They sometimes nest in specially made wedge-shaped boxes. I have provided two of these boxes in the garden but as yet the intended occupants have ignored them. On occasion a pair of Blue Tits has taken over a box, a tight squeeze for their very large brood.

Two weeks ago on looking out of my window I saw what I took to be fine snowflakes wafting down from a clear blue sky. They turned out to be scales from mature birch tree catkins, dislodged by Redpolls feeding on the ripe seeds. These tiny brown streaked finches can often be seen in bouncing flocks settling on the tops of birch and alder to feed. They are often in the company of Siskins, which visit the garden in late winter.

The snowdrops are pushing through. I like to think of them not as a winter flower, but as a very early spring flower. Life does not come to an end in winter in a wildlife garden. Cold weather lies ahead but the days are getting longer as we enter a new year. It will not be long before the first snatch of bird-song will delight the ear and raise the spirits.

February
At the beginning of the month the garden has a light covering of snow. Possibly by the middle of February the weather will be mild and damp, such are the vagaries of the British winter, variable and unpredictable. The cold dry easterly wind has desiccated the piles of fallen leaves, which had been painstakingly raked together in the autumn and swept under the hedge.

The hard frost over Christmas caused several centimetres of ice to form on the surface of the ponds. When the thaw took place several dead goldfish were found at the shallow end of the ornamental pond. This is somewhat puzzling, as at its deepest end the pond has a depth of 60 cm, sufficient for a fish to survive the hardest frost. Dead sticklebacks were reportedly found in a garden pond nearby, so this phenomenon is not confined to ornamental fish. Perhaps the fish in a torpid state did not move through the thick weed to deeper and safer water and got frozen in the ice. The mystery deepened when several dead frogs were found floating at the surface, an experience also observed by several neighbours. Another possible explanation is that ice blocks the supply of oxygen to the pond life and prevents the release of noxious gases, but the extremely low metabolic rate of hibernating amphibians and fish should exclude such an explanation. On the plus side however, as a result of the demise of the exotic fish from the actions of both frost and Heron, I have another truly wildlife pond.

The mild spell in the middle of January fooled some birds into thinking winter had ended. Tits started to examine the nest-boxes and on 8th January a male Blue Tit with fanned wings and tail was performing its bowing courting display to its mate. On 18th January a Song Thrush was in full voice. Now is the time to make sure that the nest-boxes are ready for early house hunters. A garden tool designed to remove dandelion roots from the lawn is useful for cleaning boxes. Stick the tool's twin points into the tightly packed nest material and debris and the whole noxious package with its accompanying parasites and insect larvae can be removed. If not removed, some of these beasts will become unwelcome guests on the bodies of adult birds and young alike.

Site new nest-boxes with the entrance hole facing away from the prevailing southwesterly wind and rain, and out of continuous direct sunlight. If possible situate them in such a position that it would be difficult for even the most athletically endowed cat to ambush returning adults and young when they fledge. Incidentally I noticed a tit-sized hole had been pecked into the side of one of my owl boxes. It reminded me of two recent occasions when I found tit-boxes which appeared to have been attacked by Great Spotted Woodpeckers, perhaps seeking a meal of young Blue Tits.

March

Early on the morning of 3rd February a neighbour phoned to say that there was a flock of Waxwings in his garden. By the time I had roused myself and, armed with camera and binoculars, arrived at his garden, only two were left, but it gave me opportunity to admire these dapper visitors from the north. The small flock of a dozen birds remained in our village for several days, stripping all the berries from the bushes in one garden before moving on. They finally left the village when not a single berry remained. I felt somewhat disgruntled, as they did not grace my garden with their presence. All the berries on my hawthorn, cotoneaster and holly bushes had been eaten already by a large flock of Redwings and Fieldfares. Flocks of Waxwings have been frequently observed in the proximity of supermarkets, the attraction being the berry-bearing shrubs planted when the sites are landscaped. In future years I should leave notices on my hawthorns stating 'reserved for Waxwings' – perhaps a futile gesture as invasions of these birds from Scandinavia are often at intervals of many years.

A few days ago I purchased a new bird-table and attached tit-feeders to it. They had previously been suspended outside my main window for easy viewing, a position that unfortunately necessitated frequent cleaning of the windowpane. It gave interesting views of several Long-tailed Field-mice that shared the nuts with the tits, often at the same time. I decided

42

to clean the relocated tit-feeders, finding at the bottom of the tube a hard pad of rancid peanuts that was difficult to shift. However by the expeditious use of a small screwdriver pushed through the wire mesh to loosen the debris, followed by the energetic use of a test-tube brush assisted by a stream of hot water, the feeder was cleaned. Birds, like humans, can become ill as a result of eating rancid or decayed food so bird-tables and feeders should be kept clean and hygienic. As soon as the new bird-table was charged with food the birds arrived, the tits on the feeders, the sparrows and Blackbirds on the grain, and underneath Chaffinches and Dunnocks were pecking the tiny pieces of nut and seed which fell like crumbs from a rich man's table.

February 14th was a beautiful day. It began with the cascading song of a Chaffinch, the first of the year, followed by snippets of Dunnock song and a snatch of the Robin's summer warble. There was a whiff of spring in the air, very appropriate for St Valentine's Day.

April

As I write on 2nd April, spring has not yet arrived. The air is chill and as night approaches another frost will bite. There are only three clumps of frogspawn in the ponds. The first clump was produced on 31st March. In 1994 and 1995 the frogs had spawned by the middle of March, whilst in 1993 I had a clump of spawn on 19th February. Each day as the sun warms the surface water of the ponds as many as sixty frogs begin their pre-spawning activity, but the returning chill sets in as the afternoon progresses and the cavorting amphibians become torpid and cease their courtship.

Earlier in the winter I noticed a greyish-brown Robin-sized bird hanging on a feeder. Its glossy black cap identified it as a male Blackcap, a member of the warbler family. Most Blackcaps migrate south in the autumn, but some remain, often sustained by food supplied on bird-tables. The male Blackcap and a female have been regular visitors to the nut-feeders, though latterly I have only seen the female.

At this time of year one can be forgiven for thinking that there are several new species of bird in the garden, to judge by unusual and unrecognisable birdcalls. On sighting and identification, the vocalist usually turns out to be the Great Tit, a virtuoso of many calls, although the *'teecha'* and *'churr'* calls appear to be the most frequent. These tits and the smaller Blue Tits are already inspecting the cleaned-out nestboxes. Their tiny cousin the Coal Tit whose head coloration can be compared to that of a badger, has yet to nest in one of my boxes.

It was on 3rd March that the first Siskin visited the nut-feeders, and since then they have been regular visitors, but never more than two birds at once. These birds, as also the larger Greenfinches, have not been such frequent visitors in these last two springs.

As the time for the first mowing of the lawn approaches, it would be worth considering leaving a section of it uncut. Before long, flower-stems will rise from the centre of rosettes of lawn weeds. These weeds can live for years in mown lawns without the need to flower, surviving the grass-cutter as their leaves are very close to the ground. Soon daisies, yellow cat's-ear and bright blue sheets of speedwell will appear. Unfortunately the growing grass will over-shadow these flowering plants, and so a return to mowing is necessary to avoid this happening. However if the meadow is allowed to grow uncut, further wild flowers will take advantage of the mowing amnesty and yarrows and buttercups will flower, as will the grasses. I have found that my soil is too rich, and the final stage is a heavy growth of course grasses such as cock's-foot. The experts state that long-term management includes allowing the grasses to seed, then mowing and finally removing the hay and so, over a period of many seasons, lowering the productivity of the soil. Thus the growth of coarse grasses is reduced and flowers are given a chance. I personally feel that this ambitious plan is more appropriate for the fortunate gardener who has ample land and life expectancy!

May

Summer has certainly not yet arrived on this, the first morning of May. The weather is cold and damp, windy and dull. The trees have only a touch of green on their branches, contradicting the old Mayday song, 'summer is a'comin' in: loudly sing cuckoo'. I have yet to hear this elusive summer migrant, though the air is full of the plaintive cascades of Willow Warbler song.

Primroses are out under the hedge and cuckooflowers are in bloom in the uncut damp areas near the ponds. Cowslips are bravely raising their bowed heads in clusters on the lawn. These areas I leave uncut until they have seeded. I have only cut the lawns twice this spring: the grass has been growing so slowly because of the cold weather.

A vandal has been at large in the garden, pulling up the fragile saxifrage cushions around the ponds. The culprit turned out to be a Blackbird. It was initially searching for worms, and then latterly gathering the surrounding dead vegetation as building material for its nest. The eggs in the nearby Song Thrushes' nest have hatched, the evidence being a beautiful blue eggshell with tiny black spots, which the parent had dropped some distance away from the nest to avoid disclosing its location. This pair of thrushes has been jealous of its territory, which includes the garden ponds, frequently driving away another pair of thrushes nesting nearby. The ponds contain a large number of water-snails. The thrushes find these to be just as acceptable a part of their diet as are garden snails.

The frogspawn has hatched and the tiny tadpoles have sunk to the bottom of the pond. Toads have draped their gelatinous ropes of eggs around the submerged water plants. The 'toadpoles' – is that the origin of the word tadpole? – have emerged from the jelly and are hanging free. This year the gap in time between the main frog-spawning period and that of the toads has been much shorter, due to the late spawning of the frogs.

The Collared Doves and the Woodpigeons continue to sit on their nests. One brood of young Blackbirds has fledged, in spite of the unhealthy interest taken by neighbourhood cats. The Great Tit has laid its fifth egg. A Starling has laid five glossy pale blue eggs in a large closed-fronted nest-box. Hole-nesting birds often lay white or light-coloured eggs, perhaps so that the parents can pick them out in the dark interior. As they are hidden camouflage is unnecessary.

I continue to feed the birds. I will cease to feed peanuts when the young tits hatch, as a large piece of nut fed to them by their parents could lodge in their throats. Hopefully by then a sufficient supply of caterpillars will become available as the trees come into full leaf. I have been charmed over the last few weeks by a pair of Goldfinches hanging on the nut-feeders, feeding on peanuts. Several neighbours have also reported observing this phenomenon and like me have not seen this small finch at nut feeders before. This restless bird can be easily recognised by its black, white, and red head and a broad yellow band on its wing. It has a liquid trilling song and has a fondness for the tiny seeds of thistle and dandelion. It is a very welcome visitor to the wildlife garden.

June
I can well believe that it has been the coldest May on record. The beech hedge has yet to come into full leaf and I fear it could be Midsummer Day before the ash trees are decked in full foliage.

In spite of the unseasonably chill weather the birds have been enjoying quite a successful breeding season in the garden, helped by a continuous supply of nuts, chicken-feed and kitchen waste, supplied without a break throughout the spring. Young Blackbirds and Song Thrushes have fledged and the pairs of Woodpigeons and Collared Doves have raised one young each. The Collared Doves frequently feed at the bird-table, but show little parental affection towards their one offspring, chasing it away when it attempts to feed with them. The youngster can be distinguished from its parents by the absence of a clearly defined collar mark on its neck.

On 10th May a Great Spotted Woodpecker was seen hanging on the nut-feeder, though unfortunately it did not repeat its visit. This thrush-sized bird is the commonest of our three native species of woodpecker. Its Jackdaw-sized cousin, the Green Woodpecker, has become quite scarce in our area, and its laughing 'yaffle' call only rarely heard in our wooded valleys. I have yet to see the sparrow-sized Lesser Spotted Woodpecker locally, though sightings are becoming more frequent.

On the morning of 12th May I heard what I later identified as a Garden Warbler, singing in the garden. Previously I have had difficulty distinguishing the song of this plain summer visitor from that of its near relative the Blackcap. But with a resident Garden Warbler singing every day for a week in my garden, and comparing its performance to taped tracks of bird song, I feel I have cracked the problem. Sadly all its efforts appear to have been in vain and as yet a female has not been attracted to its territory.

One nest-box contains eight young Great Tits. The parents feed on the nut-feeders themselves, but provide their young with a diet composed only of small green caterpillars. A Blue Tit is sitting on seven eggs, a late clutch compared to previous years. In another box, on 16th May, there was a single Great Tit's egg. A second egg was laid, very unusually, four days later, instead of the next day. The parent is now sitting on a full clutch. Was the first egg laid by another hen or has there been a delay in the laying process, perhaps due to the cold weather? I will wait to see if all the eggs hatch.

A brood of three recently fledged House Sparrows are being fed by their parents at the bird-table. They all have white wings, which make them very conspicuous, particularly when they flutter their wings to encourage their parents to feed them. It will be interesting to see if they survive, as nature can be cruel to deviations from the norm. Interestingly neither of the parents exhibits a single white feather.

Three species of white butterfly have been seen in the garden. The Orange-tip butterflies can be identified by the beautiful markings on the underside of the rear wings, only the male having the orange tips to its wings. The other white butterflies are the Small White and the Green-veined White. The latter can be distinguished from the former by the greyish-green veins on the underside of its yellowish hind wings. The Orange-tip and the Green-veined White lay their eggs on crucifers, including hedge garlic and cuckooflower. You will only see fully grown Orange-tip caterpillars on their own, as they have an unsociable tendency to cannibalism.

July

A few weeks ago we moved straight from cold winter to hot dry summer weather. Where have our springs gone? The flowers and trees have certainly made up for lost time and June has 'burst out all over'. The young tits have fledged, although in two cases a runt of the brood has been left dead in the noisome remains of the nest debris.

I sighted a pair of Spotted Flycatchers on the morning of 29th May, but my expectations were prematurely raised. They flitted about for a day or two but gave no indication as to where they were building their nest. On three previous occasions attempts at rearing a family had ended in failure. Nestlings had died or eggs had been taken. They had always nested in a climbing rose growing on the south wall of the house. The only place I had left unchecked was an artificial House Martin nest close to our front door, and sure enough on examination a neat, deep, cupped nest was found. The flycatcher subsequently laid five eggs and sat tight in spite of frequent to-ing and fro-ing at the door. On returning from a few days holiday I was sad to find that the nest had been attacked and the eggs or young had gone. The guilty party could be Carrion Crows or Magpies. I sometimes feel that there is a jinx on Spotted Flycatchers trying to nest in the garden. Even though one is pragmatic enough to know it is nature's way, one is sentimental enough to feel a sense of loss.

Now the warm evenings have arrived, the catch in my moth-trap has become more numerous and diverse. Two particularly spectacular species have been hawkmoths. One is the Poplar Hawkmoth, with two 'eyes' on its hindwings to deter prospective predators. The other is the rose-pink Elephant Hawkmoth, named for its caterpillar's extendable proboscis, which supposedly resembles an elephant's trunk. At night it can be found feeding on the foliage of rosebay willowherb. During the latter part of May several large beetles were caught in the moth trap. These are cockchafers or maybugs. I remember that these heavy-bodied insects giving a hefty smack on the cheek when riding a motorbike at night in early summer.

Both Common and Palmate Newts have spawned and their fish-like larvae are feeding on the wealth of tiny pond creatures, including Daphnia or water fleas. These tiny crustaceans are swimming in dense swarms in the gin-clear water of the big pond. The quality of the water may have been improved by the immersion last summer of bales of straw. We have passed the longest day and hopefully we are in for a warm sunny summer with enough rain to keep the garden fresh and luxuriant for the insects and butterflies to come.

August
During the last few weeks, the area where I grow soft fruit has become a venue for Blackbirds and Song Thrushes. These resident birds spend most of the day stripping gooseberries, raspberries and blackcurrants from the bushes. As well as devouring them themselves, they feed the energy-rich food to their clamouring ever-hungry young, which follow them everywhere, begging with quivering wings. I have already picked my share of the fruit for desert and to make wine and am willing to let the garden birds have the rest. The use of netting to protect fruit from feeding birds can result in them getting trapped, perhaps with fatal

results. As always in dry summers, earthworms – their other main food source – have become difficult to find. They have burrowed deep to avoid desiccation.

The ponds have become covered with a green film of duckweed. I frequently remove quantities of it to allow sunlight to reach the submerged plants and increase photosynthesis, and thus to produce more oxygen. The regular removal of weed reduces the chemical content of the pond water, which has become concentrated by evaporation and subsequent topping up with tap water. Last week I was pleased to see a blue needle wafting over the pond surface. It was a Common Blue Damselfly, a cousin of the larger and more robust dragonflies.

Four species of large colourful butterfly visit the garden. Early this summer there was an invasion of Painted Ladies, frequent visitors to the wildlife garden. They lay their eggs on thistles and can produce a home-grown generation, with a richer tone to its colouring compared to the faded livery of its migrant parents. They will not survive our winter. However Small Tortoiseshells, Peacocks and possibly Red Admirals can hibernate, though Red Admirals are augmented by large numbers of migrants each summer. The caterpillars of these three butterflies feed on nettle leaves. They prefer young, fresh growth in a sunny position. Such an area of vegetation is a 'must' in the wildlife garden!

September

At the beginning of September the earliest indicators of autumn are increasingly perceptible. The nights are drawing in, and the wistful winter song of the Robin can be heard, more noticeable because of the absence of other bird song.

After a summer break of several months I began feeding the garden birds again. The first visitors to the nut-feeders were Greenfinches and Great Tits, while House Sparrows pecked at the chicken feed on the bird-table. One of the sparrows had white wing feathers, a survivor of the brood fledged in the spring. To avoid predation by cats, birds should not be fed on the ground, and the bird-table should be placed more than a cat-leap from the cover of a hedge or long grass.

The Russian vine is covered with swathes of tiny white flowers and festooned with several species of butterfly, particularly Red Admirals. The buddleia have similarly been graced with nectaring lepidoptera. These bushes have grown quite tall and I have had difficulty photographing the insects in close-up while balanced on the top of a stepladder. After flowering I will cut them down to head height to facilitate easier photography next year. Yesterday I was overjoyed to see two Peacock butterflies on the same flower spike. For many years the sight of even a singleton was a rarity in my garden.

Two species of blue butterfly may visit the garden. The one most likely to be seen is the Common Blue, the female of which is partly brown. Its larval food plant is bird's-foot trefoil, so-called because its thin pea-like seedpods resemble a bird's foot. It is also called 'bacon-and-eggs' because of the reddish-yellow colour of its petals. The other 'blue' is the tiny Holly Blue. As yet it has not been seen in my garden, but in some years it is found in the Carlisle area. The wings of the Holly Blue are blue or brownish-blue on the upper surface and silver with tiny black dots on the lower surface. It flies at some distance from the ground, unlike the low flying Common Blue. The Holly Blue usually has two broods a year, but in the north may only have one. The eggs are laid on holly flowers in the spring and the second brood is laid on ivy flowers in the summer.

For several weeks this summer I have been visiting areas in the south noted for their butterflies. I was fortunate to find and photograph several of our most rare species. It was the abundance of butterflies that impressed me, particularly on unimproved downland, doubtless of course helped by the hot sunny weather. These idyllic scenes reminded me of a child's early picture book, with bright flowers and a shimmering cloud of gaudy butterflies above. How nice it would be if more of our countryside could be like a children's painting of a rural scene, with fewer '-cides' being used. It may be a Utopian pipedream but at least we can make an effort by developing our gardens for wildlife to make miniature Utopias – larger ones if our neighbours follow suit. We should allow wild plants such as grasses, cresses and nettles to grow as food plants for the caterpillars, and flowering plants such as Michaelmas daises and buddleia as nectar sources for the adult butterflies and moths.

October

As I write on 26th September a fine drizzle is falling, the first rain for several weeks. The lawn is parched and turning brown and the soil has the consistency of snuff. The worms have retreated deep into the ground to avoid desiccation. The only one I did find was coiled in a tight knot, reminiscent of a flayed golf ball. Blackbirds, denied their staple diet of earthworms, have taken their revenge on the ripened plums and soft-fleshed early eating apples.

One of my Victoria plum trees collapsed recently, the brittle wood splintering under the unaccustomed weight of ripening fruit. This is the first year my trees have produced a heavy crop. I believe this to be due to the extremely late season, delaying the flowering and setting of the fruit until after the frosts had finished. In previous years early flowering has always been followed by a rogue late frost with resultant damage to the setting fruit.

Even though recent springs and early summers have been cold, our high summers, arriving belatedly this year, have been hot, dry and sunny. One possible effect of this climatic change has been the steady movement north of several species of butterfly. The Comma is a good example of a butterfly moving into our area from the south. It is resident and breeding in the south of Cumbria, but in the last two years individuals have been sighted in gardens in the north of the county, including the Carlisle area. This orange-brown butterfly bears some similarity to a Small Tortoiseshell, but with a ragged edge to its wings. When its wings are closed the Comma looks like a dead leaf, with on its hindwing the distinctive white comma mark that gives the butterfly its name. Hopefully in 1997 more of us will see these uniquely shaped butterflies in our gardens. We may also see their caterpillars, which resemble bird droppings, feeding on their main food source, nettles.

On 15th September, for a few minutes, I was honoured by the presence in my garden of a large dragonfly with apple-green markings. This was a Southern Hawker, another species that has moved north into our area over the last few years. Lately it has frequented gardens locally and I like to think in the future it might breed in my ponds.

Some weeks ago my attention was drawn to the spectacle of a large number of wasps crawling slowly over my car, which was parked under some silver birch. On closer examination they were seen to be feeding on the tiny spots of honeydew secreted by aphids feeding on the leaves above. I hope the wasps were not too miffed when I decided a car wash was required.

November

One evening recently, as dusk fell, my attention was drawn to a cacophony of sound coming from the high hawthorn hedge. The hooting call of a Tawny Owl when heard in the distance sounds melodious, even wistful, but at close quarters it can be quite unsettling, until one identifies its owner. In addition to the *'hoo, hoo, hoo-oo-oo'* call there was a *'kee-wick'* sound. These two calls heard together equate to the *'tu-whit, tu-who'* used in literature to represent the call of an owl. In fact two owls are involved, the *'kee-wick'* call from one owl, often the female, being answered by the hoot of her mate. A pair of Tawny Owls nest each spring in an owl box in our village nature reserve nearby and I hope that a pair of their young will take up residence in one of two boxes I have placed in my garden. Owls are very early nesters. They often establish territories well in advance of their nesting season, so they can be very vocal at this time of year.

The recent gales have stripped most of the remaining leaves from the trees. Many of them have blown into the ponds. When removing the leaves I try to avoid disturbing the pond bottom where by now the frogs will have begun their hibernation. The newts and toads have left the ponds and will be well hidden below ground in the rockery.

I never burn garden rubbish but pile it under the trees to provide shelter for small rodents and insects. It is also the place where the garden Hedgehogs hibernate. Hopefully none of these urchins will have been unfortunate enough to choose a Guy Fawkes bonfire in which to begin their hibernation. It is always advisable before setting light to garden rubbish to check that there will be no victims of incineration.

December

As I write at the end of November, the view of the village is still partly obscured by leaves, because the large beech tree outside my window has retained its foliage. This is a repeat of 1995 when many trees, notably oak and beech, held on to their leaves well into autumn and early winter. This is I believe a reflection of a seasonal shift to warmer autumns and colder springs.

The hedges have produced the usual fruits of autumn. The blackberries have all been eaten, though less palatable fruits such as sloes and holly still festoon the bushes. I have noticed the territorial behaviour of Blackbirds, feeding on the dwindling supply of hawthorn berries. Each bird has a bush or stretch of hedge that it regards as its own feeding station, and any other Blackbird that trespasses into its territory is given short shrift and chased off. The 'owner' then resumes feeding on its length of berried hedge.

At this time of year when tidying the garden, particularly when digging over a patch of soil, gardeners are often accompanied by a bright-eyed, orange-breasted bird which hops down to within a few inches of our feet to pick up a disinterred worm. This behaviour could have developed recently, since man began to garden, but my theory is that the habit of close association with a large energetic mammal began a long time ago with rooting forest pigs. The Robin, a woodland bird, fed on the worms that the pigs unearthed from the soft soil of the forest floor. This relationship was later transferred to human gardeners whose activities, if not necessarily behaviour, are similar to those of pigs. It is fitting that we should end with a discussion on the feeding habits of the Robin, a traditional bird of Christmas.

Honeysuckle

January

This morning, 3rd January, the weather is bitterly cold and the garden is rock-hard with frost. All the fruits of the hedgerow have been stripped from the bushes by hungry birds. Not even a holly berry is left! Now is the time for helping the garden birds to survive the winter, as any Christmas leftovers put out for them will have been consumed, often at a frenzied pace, by flocks of garrulous Starlings.

I add grain to the household scraps placed on the bird-table. The table has a pitched roof to prevent rain from spoiling the grain and snow from burying it. During a hard frost it is advisable to offer a continuous supply of drinking water to the birds. Stop ice from forming by periodically adding a quantity of lukewarm water.

To the north of Carlisle lives an expert in making bird feeders. He makes tit-feeders by rolling half-inch galvanised metal mesh into the shape of a cylinder. As the squares overlap each other the apertures become smaller so retaining the enclosed peanuts. The caps and bases of the cylinders are the lids of coffee-jars, the bases being drilled with small holes to allow drainage. Another piece of feeding apparatus developed by this inventor is the 'slice-holder'. This piece of technology again uses half-inch mesh, bent to form a cuboid, roughly eight by five inches and half an inch deep, just the right size to accommodate a medium slice of bread. I have found toast to be more successful as the birds can easily peck crumbs off the brittle slice through the mesh. Considerable entertainment can be had watching the antics of tits and other small birds as they hang from the slice-holder. If the slice of bread had been placed on the bird-table a crow or seagull could remove the whole piece in a split-second.

February

Recently there has been talk concerning the increase in numbers of birds of prey and the effect this has on other wildlife, particularly songbirds. It is a fact that for a raptor to be successful, there must be an ample and consistent supply of its prey, if that prey is its only food source. Therefore it could be said that an increase in the Sparrowhawk population, for example, could be indicative of a healthy population of garden birds. If domestic cats existed in a completely wild state then their numbers would be controlled by the availability of prey. However, as people feed cats, an artificially high density of this carnivore is maintained, much greater than it would be in the wild. Cats, even though domesticated and fed by their owners, still retain their hunting and killing instincts. In spite of being a cat-lover I am realistic enough to acknowledge the havoc cats can wreak on the garden bird population. Young birds, either in the nest or just fledged, are most at risk. Cats are not usually contained, and are therefore difficult to control.

Some weeks ago, when moving a piece of furniture indoors, I disturbed a Small Tortoiseshell butterfly. This insect is one of several species of butterfly that hibernate through the winter as adults. I placed the butterfly in a secluded corner of the garage where the temperature is consistently cold. This was to encourage it to again become torpid and resume hibernation, so avoiding it using up food reserves in futile activity and jeopardising its chances of survival. Recently I have heard two accounts of what appear to be hibernating Red Admiral butterflies. It is thought that a few of these handsome black, red and white insects can survive our winters, though mainly in the south. Most adults seen in the spring are migrants.

March

Today, 3rd March, there is a gelatinous clump of frogspawn in the large pond. When I checked my diary for last year I found that the first garden record for frogspawn that year was 30th March, nearly one month later! This must have been a reflection of last year's very late spring, caused by weeks of continuous cold easterly winds. This year, in contrast, after a cold dry January we have enjoyed a mild, though very wet, February. The ponds are full of frogs, and soon they will be nearly choked with spawn.

Earlier in the year I trawled large quantities of leaves and sludge from the bottom of the deep end of the large pond. Only one somnolent frog was dredged up with the evil-smelling slime. However, fifty frogs have suddenly appeared on the surface of the weedy middle and shallow ends of the pond. It appears that the frogs have not hibernated in the deepest part, but the shallower weedy parts of the pond, perhaps making them more vulnerable during protracted periods of hard frost.

Nothing raises the spirits more than the increasing chorus of bird song. Some birds, such as tits and Robins, can often be heard singing throughout the year but many songbirds begin their spring singing around about St Valentine's Day. I heard the repeated refrain of the Song Thrush on 5th February, the fluting song of the Blackbird on 14th, closely followed the next day by the cheery cascade of the Chaffinch. I am currently fortunate in having two male Song Thrushes singing at either end of the garden, belying the general trend in the reduction in numbers of this vocal harbinger of spring. Each year two pairs build their nests and lay their eggs, but are frequently unsuccessful in fledging their young, mainly due to the attentions of the local cats, crows and Magpies. In my experience Song Thrushes tend to nest in evergreens such as holly or cupressus, while

Blackbirds frequently choose a deciduous bush or climbing shrub. I also find that Blackbirds tend to build later than Song Thrushes. The Song Thrushes are prospecting for nest sites and chasing each other around the garden. Are they mates or rivals?

There is a beautiful display of snowdrops and crocuses in the garden and the daffodils are much further advanced than this time last year. Some lesser celandine flowers were out at the end of February, a month earlier than last year. Frogs are croaking loudly in the ponds. Spring is waiting in the wings but will only be fully on stage when the summer migrants arrive on the wing in April.

April

The weather has been very mild and spring like. During this balmy period all the frogs spawned in a very few days, and soon after they all left the pond *en masse*. I have received various reports in similar vein. One day the ponds are full of frogs and the next day not one is to be seen! This behaviour I would guess is due to the mild and damp weather conditions, good both for spawning and for amphibians to leave the water and begin feeding. Spawning during early spring in recent years has been interrupted by long periods of cold weather, causing egg laying to be protracted and delaying the exodus of the adults from the water.

Two pairs of Blackbirds and one pair of Song Thrushes are nesting and a Robin has built its nest in an ivy-covered bank below the hawthorn hedge. Some weeks ago a pair of Carrion Crows was perched on a silver birch tree, wrenching at twigs on the topmost branches, finally breaking them off and flying to their bulky nest in a tall oak in the adjacent field, to add to its structure.

Insects are appearing in the garden. Large bumblebees are droning around the yellow male catkins of the sallow, collecting both pollen and nectar. A Small Tortoiseshell butterfly has emerged from hibernation. Several species of moth have been attracted to my light trap in the garden overnight. Two of the more numerous are the Small and Common Quakers, insects of subdued coloration as their name signifies. A somewhat cryptic but beautifully marked moth, the Early Grey, comes to a moth light in large numbers, especially if the food plant of its caterpillar, honeysuckle, is in the garden.

Any butterfly enthusiast who enjoys the spectacle of these colourful insects in their garden may have their interest in the Lepidoptera increased by extending their knowledge to moths, the night-flying cousins of butterflies. They are not all clothes-devouring pests! Many have interesting shapes and their wings have different patterns, such as the so-called carpet moths. They do not live in carpets but the patterns on their wings resemble what might be found on a carpet. Some day-flying moths, such as the burnets, are very colourful. As well as the use of moth traps, night-flying moths can be attracted by 'sugaring': painting a mixture of an alcoholic beverage and sugar onto fence-posts or tree-trunks. Strips of cloth can be hung from branches after being soaked in this intoxicating liquor. It is surprising how many species of moth can be found in a quite modest garden. After about ten years I had recorded two hundred and fifty-three species of macro moths compared to thirteen species of butterflies. The term 'macro moths' is loosely applied to larger moths. I also recorded about twenty species of tiny moths, micro moths. Learning about the food plants of the various species of caterpillar can develop one's interest further.

The indicators of spring creep hesitantly into the garden. The glossy green cushions of lesser celandines with their yellow star-shaped flowers contrast with the pale blue of delicate violets, almost overlooked in the hedge bottom. I am waiting impatiently for the first Swallow of the year. That one swallow will not make a summer, but at least we will know that spring has truly arrived!

May

The weather suddenly turned warm on 1st May. Orange-tip and Green-veined White butterflies were flitting around the flowering hedge garlic and cuckooflower, their larval food plants. For the last two weeks a solitary Swallow was occupying in forlorn isolation its ancestral nesting site in the barn belonging to the village shopkeeper, but now it has been joined by a flock of twittering compatriots. It is the height of the breeding season for the resident garden birds. One nest-box contains seven eggs of a Great Tit and another has an incomplete clutch of four Blue Tit eggs. My experience is that Blue Tits have larger clutches than their close relatives, the larger Great Tits. Yet again the resident pair of Coal Tits have not used a nest-box. I believe they are nesting in a position inaccessible to me, under brush at the hedge roots. The two pairs of Blackbirds are sitting on eggs in nests only about 20 metres apart.

The young of one of the resident pairs of Song Thrushes have already fledged and the strident scolding alarm notes of their parents can be frequently heard signalling the presence of a prowling cat. Each year at least one and often two pairs of Song Thrushes nest in my quite modest garden.

A Woodpigeon is sitting on its pair of glossy white eggs quite high in a cupressus, its heavy body loudly crashing off its nest when disturbed. Its smaller and daintier relative the Collared Dove is at present building its frail platform of a nest in an adjacent evergreen. I have been watching it make a futile attempt to wrench off pieces of Russian vine, to no avail. It stubbornly continued for some time, obviously preferring living material to dead twigs that it could have collected easily from the ground.

A few weeks ago I had an interesting visitor to the garden. I watched it hovering like a tiny hummingbird in front of primrose plants, taking nectar from their flowers. It is a plump, furry bumblebee-like fly, appropriately called a bee-fly. This species is the Dark-edged Bee-fly and is the only common and widespread member of this small group of insects.

I heard a bird sing in the garden today. It is either a Garden Warbler or a Blackcap, but unless I see the singer I cannot be positive which. Some birdwatchers profess to be able to identify confidently which of these two species of warbler is singing. When challenged and put to the test they may be found to be wrong. The usual retort is "Well! I get it right fifty percent of the time!" Garden Warbler or Blackcap, it's a privilege to have either of these beautiful songsters in the wildlife garden.

June

Several misfortunes have beset my resident Blue and Great Tits during the last few weeks. One nest-box contained a clutch of ten Blue Tit eggs but was left un-brooded for some days. I had assumed it had been deserted and was on the point of removing the nest and eggs to avoid disease, when the hen bird began to sit again. However on returning from a week's holiday I was dismayed to find the nest deserted and containing an infertile egg and one dead nestling. What had happened to the other young? Another Blue Tit laid four eggs in a nest-box and then abandoned them. In this case, instead of returning to incubate them, she made another nest in an adjacent box and laid a further seven eggs. Are these seven eggs the delayed remaining seven eggs of a clutch of eleven? The hen is sitting tight and hopefully she will rear this depleted brood.

A pair of Great Tits was feeding a brood of seven youngsters when I went away. On my return I was saddened to find the cold bodies of two dead nestlings at the bottom of the nest-box. What had happened to the other young? Had they slowly starved and their parents removed them when they had died? If the box had been attacked, what creature had been the perpetrator? Great Spotted Woodpeckers enjoy a meal of young tits, but always leave their calling card, a splintered hole in the side of the box.

I feel that these unfortunate happenings have at least in part been exacerbated by the capricious nature of the weather. Endless days of cool winds were followed by periods with night frosts, interspersed with occasional short periods of wet and thundery weather, not conducive to efficient insect gathering and chick rearing. This is a disappointment after the promising warm weather of early spring. However we are now experiencing a period of warm sunny weather. The Swallows are flying low over the garden. I have noticed a reduction in the numbers of House Martins and Swifts this year.

After my disappointment at the death of all the frogspawn in early spring, there is some compensation in the wriggling brood of toad tadpoles – or should I say 'toadpoles' – that have, perhaps inadvisably, decided to spend their early days in the one pond that contains ornamental fish. This is a good test to see whether the goldfish will enjoy eating these young amphibians as much as they enjoy eating their cousins, the frog tadpoles. When examining a cluster of 'toadpoles' in the cup of my palm, I also just managed to perceive some minute hair-like creatures. On examining them under the binocular microscope, I identified them as miniscule goldfish just emerged from their eggs. Some days previously I had observed their parents chasing each other through the Canadian waterweed, obviously spawning. I bought these fish in the winter and have hardly seen them since, but they appear to have fed well at the bottom of the pond.

Now is the time of year when the moth-trap begins to yield some more interesting finds. No new species as yet, but the huge Poplar Hawkmoth with its large vibrating wings, heavy body, and clinging feet, has made a surprisingly exotic appearance. Several Maybugs or Cockchafers are caught each night. Their appearance can cause some alarm to small children. The release of the contents of the trap must be done in such a way as to avoid every garden bird thinking that it is an extension of the bird-table, with a helping of Hebrew Character, a lunch of Larch Carpet, or a supper of Silver-Y. The lighter moths flutter into the bushes. The heavier ones I thrust into the deep undergrowth. Recently however a Maybug flopped onto the lawn and a male Blackbird, feeding three newly fledged young, dismembered the unfortunate insect in seconds and provided one clamorous youngster with dainty morsels of fast food.

July

As I write at the end of 'flaming June', I feel that the adjective flaming is descriptive of one's feeling of frustration with the dull, wet and unseasonably cold weather that we are experiencing.

The unsettled weather, however, is encouraging the peregrinations of wandering pond-snails, which leave the pond in huge numbers, much to the gratification of the local thrushes. One pair of Song Thrushes is feeding a brood of newly fledged young, mostly on pond-snails. In our immediate neighbourhood we have a healthy population of this attractive songbird, which belies the reported decrease in their numbers generally. I believe their success is partly due to the continuous supply of large pond-snails. They use these as a substitute for their normal diet of land-snails, which are scarce in my garden. The decrease nationwide may be partly caused by the increase in the domestic cat population, which has an adverse effect on newly fledged and near flightless young, and also by the use of certain brands of slug-pellet. The adult birds are poisoned when they feed on slugs and snails killed by the pellets.

When examining a nest-box on my garage wall I received an unexpected sting on my hand. I had unwittingly invaded the space of a colony of Tree Wasps. These social insects had built their papery, roughly spherical nest in the branches of a *Clematis montana*. These wasps can be quite aggressive if they think that their nest is threatened, so I decided to leave it well alone. At this time of the year their presence is beneficial as they kill large numbers of insect pests. I make certain that any visitor is aware of their presence so that they can give the nest a wide berth.

Two small butterflies that may pay a visit in high summer are the Small Copper – provide sorrel for its caterpillars – and the Large Skipper. Two 'brown' butterflies are now on the wing, the Meadow Brown, and the much darker Ringlet, characterised by rings on its hindwings. This last butterfly is rare or absent in the south of the county but common round Carlisle. One may be fortunate to have a colony of Common Blues if one has patches of bird's-foot trefoil, the larval food-plant.

August

The weather lately has been warm and sultry with plenty of rain to keep the ground soft. Blackbirds and thrushes can easily obtain a ready supply of earthworms, denied to them in recent dry summers. As I write a recently fledged Song Thrush is being fed by its attentive parent. It is likely to be from a second brood of one of the two pairs of resident thrushes.

Once again the Spotted Flycatchers have been unsuccessful in raising a brood. This pair of late summer migrants built themselves a nest on top of a tit-box, disregarding the open-fronted boxes specifically provided for them or for robins. Four brown-blotched eggs were laid, though one subsequently broke and was discarded. The hen began sitting on about 4th July, when we went away on holiday. She was still on the nest on 23rd. That means incubation had lasted nineteen days, six days longer than a normal incubation period. Something was amiss! The problem was solved when she finally left the nest a day later and I examined the eggs. In each egg was a fairly well developed but dead and decaying chick. I had been told that there had been a violent thunderstorm in the area on 13th July, nine days after incubation had begun, and I assume the nest had been soaked, the eggs chilled, and the embryo chicks killed. If only the nest had been built *inside* one of the dry, sheltered, nest-boxes provided! I feel that there is a jinx on Spotted Flycatchers in my garden. This is the fourth year that a clutch or a brood has died. On a brighter note, it appears that these demure and secretive little birds are increasing in numbers. In the garden of a close neighbour is a pair of flycatchers that has recently reared

Magpie Moth

a brood successfully in a halved coconut-shell, put in the garden as a feeding station.

This is the quietest time of the year with respect to bird song. Most birds have finished nesting and are mute, and as yet the Robins have not begun their autumn laments. The froglets and toadlets have left the ponds, the smaller, darker, toadlets crawling along on spindly legs.

The warm humid evenings of the last few weeks have produced large catches in the moth-traps. Different species of moth fly at different times of the year. Every gardener is familiar with the Large Yellow Underwing, which is flushed out from the lawn edges when cutting the grass, showing a flash of bright yellow. A conspicuous moth now flying is the Magpie Moth, whose caterpillars feed on blackcurrant leaves.

September

The hot dry weather of the last few weeks has changed to a more typical unsettled period of wind and rain. This summery weather was beneficial to butterflies, particularly Peacocks. In fact if we named our years after these insects 1997 would be the year of the Peacock butterfly, just as 1995 was the year of the Red Admiral and 1996 the year of the Painted Lady. Accompanying the Peacocks on the buddleia have been several Red Admirals, some Small Tortoiseshells but as yet not a single Painted Lady.

I counted one hundred and fifty Peacocks on a single walk in a nearby wood. These dark exotic-looking insects have those beautiful Peacock-tail 'eyes' on both fore- and hindwings. They look as if they had been painted by an artist. I also encountered my first Comma butterfly for this wood. As yet they have not visited my garden.

Other insects that appear to have benefited from the recent hot spell are several species of hoverfly. They have reached plague proportions in my garden and have invaded the conservatory in swarms. These wasp-like insects are completely harmless but can cause panic among the uninitiated, resulting in flailing arms and talk of being attacked by 'Hornets'.

For several evenings the garden was invaded by a swarm – or is it a flock? – of bats. I usually have one or two of these tiny flying mammals hawking after insects, but never before this number. I saw as many as six on the wing at one time, though I think there were several more. They seemed to interact with each other. Whether it had some sexual or social dimension I do not know. I assume these bats were Pipistrelles, our commonest species. However their presence did not adversely affect the size of the catch in my moth-trap, which contained several species new to my garden. One was a male Vapourer moth with ochre-red wings, each with a comma-shaped white spot. It is unusual in that the flightless female never leaves her cocoon, where pairing with the day-flying male takes place.

Parts of the hedge have been engulfed by triffid-like strands of briar, which are now producing the first luscious sweet blackberries. I am entertained by the antics of a family of Blackbirds. Each leaps up to the fruit and descends with a blackberry in its beak, like a jack-in-a-box. Blackbirds have seriously attacked the early-ripening apples this year. Many, still attached to the branches, are nothing but a stalk and skin.

The summer peak is over. The Swifts have long gone, soon to be followed by the Swallows and Martins. A touch of autumn is in the air. Michaelmas daisies will soon be in flower, hopefully attracting more late-summer butterflies.

October

Most days have been warm and sunny with little wind and rain. Even the Swallows are reluctant to leave and are hawking about the village after the still-abundant flying insects.

The weather has been ideal for the early autumn tasks of tidying the borders, hedge cutting and tree pruning. This latter activity I am having to pursue vigorously and ruthlessly this autumn. Indications of the necessity of this operation have become increasingly obvious over the last two years. Twelve years ago I planted saplings of birch, sallow and wild cherry to provide screening, cover and a source of food for the garden birds. However, last year the water-lilies produced only one flower and this year none at all. The lawn surrounding the ponds became mossy and damp. The ponds were becoming too shaded. Deterioration of water quality and a lowering of temperature had taken place. This may have been a factor contributory to the failure to hatch of most of the frogspawn this spring. Some days ago, a tree surgeon arrived to lower the height of the trees on the south and west sides of the garden to allow more light to reach the ponds. It is a pity that trees and hedges cannot be 'stopped' at just the right height and thickness.

I am always happy to record a first in the wildlife garden. Last year my horse-chestnut tree produced its first spike of flowers. This year I noticed the first green spiky fruit at the top of the twelve-year old tree. Perhaps next year there will be enough to provide ammunition for a conker fight.

November

October has been a changeover month. Swallows and Martins have left the village to be replaced by flocks of Redwings closely followed by their relatives, the Fieldfares. The luscious bunches of elderberries have already disappeared and the hawthorn berries are rapidly being devoured by these ravenous Scandinavian thrushes.

The weather has been noticeably colder in the last few days. I have begun to feed the garden birds regularly as the wild foods have become depleted. Great, Blue and Coal Tits hang from the feeders and Collared Doves peck at the grain placed on the bird-table. Prior to initiating winter feeding, I gave the feeders and tables an autumn clean. I noticed with disgust the debris on the bird-table, the remains of food rejected by the birds during the summer glut. This noisome mess contained the larvae of flies and an accompanying creep of woodlice. This unsavoury cocktail I diligently removed and gave the table a good scrape down. Birds, like humans, require hygiene at their feeding stations.

The clocks have gone back, the dark evenings are here, but during the next five dark months the garden can become an oasis for feathered refugees from the surrounding increasingly barren countryside. If a well-stocked bird-table is kept the reward will be an ever-changing panorama of tits, thrushes and finches.

December
Early last month I looked out onto the garden and caught sight of an insect zooming and hovering over the ponds. It was a large dragonfly, a female Southern Hawker. I have only recently become interested in these colourful ancient creatures and have been trying to acquire a working knowledge in the identification of our more common species. The Southern Hawker, as its name suggests, is found predominantly in the south of Britain. However during the last few years it has moved north into our area. It can be seen along with its cousin the Common Hawker near lakes and even over garden ponds. It is a large dragonfly with predominantly apple-green markings. Only about a dozen kinds occur in our area and about half of these are the thin damselflies or 'Devil's Darning Needles.' Amongst the commonest species in this group are the Common Blue and the Large Red Damselflies, identified by their colour.

Final leaf-fall came late this autumn due to the recent protracted period of calm weather. As I was raking the leaves on the lawn in late November I became aware of a Song Thrush singing. The time was 4.00 pm, and it continued to sing until 4.20 pm, at which time it was dark. At daybreak the following day it began to sing again though not for such a long period. The weather had been sunny for these two days and perhaps the bird had been conned into thinking the day-length was increasing, a phenomenon that can trigger singing in early spring.

All the raked leaves, along with cut branches, I have heaped in piles under the trees and against the hedge. Hopefully these retreats will provide shelter for small rodents, shrews and Hedgehogs. They will also be a breeding ground for minibeasts and thus a food source for both mammals and birds.

Earlier today I watched in amazement as a Sparrowhawk took a bath in the pond. It was standing on the submerged netting, placed over the pond to intercept fallen leaves, and it was splashing away just as a Blackbird would. After some minutes it tried to take off but it had caught its long curved claws in the fine netting. However after some frantic flapping it managed to escape, no worse for its ordeal. A pond is an essential constituent in the wildlife garden, not just because of the living creatures it contains, but also because of the interesting visitors it attracts.

Fieldfare

January

The New Year started with mild, windy weather. Our only cold snap of the winter so far was back in December, when on the morning of 2nd we awoke to a light covering of snow. The colder weather was marked by the arrival of a flock of migrant Fieldfares. They smothered the hawthorn hedge and quickly demolished its crop of haws.

I reported last month hearing a Song Thrush singing at the end of November, but I have not heard it since. However its cousin, the larger Mistle Thrush, I have heard singing on several occasions, notably 13th and 29th December, straddling the shortest day of the year. Even though the weather has been mild, there has been a steady stream of black-headed Great Tits, the smaller blue-headed Blue Tits, and diminutive black-headed Coal Tits to the nut-feeders. A few Chaffinches hop about, pecking at the fallen pieces of peanuts lying under the bird-table, accompanied by the occasional Dunnock.

Though it is the middle of winter, now is the time to consider providing more nest-boxes for hole-nesting garden birds. Tits use a closed box with an entrance hole the size of a 10-pence piece, 2.25 cm diameter maximum, for Blue Tits and Coal Tits. Great Tits need a slightly larger hole, at 3 cm diameter. Ideally the box should have a base 12 cm by 12 cm square and up to 20 cm high. Robins, Spotted Flycatchers and sometimes Wrens prefer an open-fronted box, the same size as a tit-box but with the top half of the front removed. Wedge-shaped boxes can be supplied for Treecreepers.

Though the coldest weather is still to come, the days are getting longer and the white-tipped shoots of snowdrops are pushing with determination through the soil. There is no halt to nature's cycle in the wildlife garden.

February

This morning, the weather is perfect: cold, with a touch of frost in the air, but calm and sunny. There is an almost imperceptible lengthening of the days. My feeling of well-being is accentuated by what I believe to be the spring song of a Robin, a foretaste of the breeding season to come. During the last few nights, the ghostly calls of Tawny Owls have been heard, as these early nesters define their breeding territories. These sounds, along with visual indicators such as the flowering of snowdrops and crocuses, are milestones on a steady progression through the winter towards spring and its chorus of bird song.

Three species of finch are usually regular visitors to feeders and the bird-table. The most common visitor is the Chaffinch, which either feeds on the table or pecks the tiny pieces of nut that fall below the feeders. Its two more acrobatic cousins, the Greenfinch and the Siskin, hang from the feeders, the Siskin often head downwards. Both these finches are greenish in colour, but the Greenfinch is sparrow-sized whilst the Siskin is the size of a Blue Tit. The latter finch has yet to visit my garden this winter, though usually they do so in late winter and early spring. Other birds seen hanging from feeders, and which have only recently developed this habit, are Robins and Long-tailed Tits.

Some days have been so warm that butterflies have been seen on the wing. These are mostly Small Tortoiseshells or Peacocks, but one could be on the lookout for Red Admirals. They are usually migratory but may be hibernating in our area. Also one might see the Comma, which is colonising north Cumbria, albeit in small numbers.

March

The arrival of a dusting of snow and a chilling northerly wind reminded us that winter is still here. We had been deceived into believing that winter had ended, with some very mild weather and the blooming of spring flowers. Daffodils have been flowering well before the beginning of Lent, belying their other name, Lent Lilies. Wild flowers such as lesser celandines, dandelions and daisies have been opening their petals in the warm sunshine.

Song Thrushes chased each other around the garden, whether in courtship or as a result of competition between rival males I do not know. The following day, three cock thrushes were singing within the confines of the garden and two others were heard within a hundred metres or so. This local concentration may have been caused in part by the removal of a nearby hedgerow, causing a paucity of suitable nesting sites.

Last month on the 9th February it was very mild and frogs were active in the large pond, having hibernated in the mud at the bottom. The following day other frogs were attempting to enter the water, indicating that some had hibernated elsewhere. Neighbours had reported frogspawn on Valentine's Day, but it was not until 22nd February that I found eight clumps of jelly in the ponds. In the middle of the month two toads were present in the large pond, along with their coils of spawn. Toad-spawn reminds me of French knitting, the enclosed eggs like a double string, completely different from the jellyfish-like clumps of frogspawn.

I have not had the variety of birds visiting the bird-table this season as in previous years. There have been few Greenfinches and not a single Siskin to date. A friend reports that he has seen a Treecreeper on a nut-feeder and has had a visit from a Brambling to his bird-table. This close relative of the Chaffinch is a winter visitor and is not dissimilar in size and appearance to its native cousin. It can be identified in flight by its white rump.

I have already given the lawn an early cut, being careful to mow round the crinkly lobes of cowslip leaves. Signs of spring include the pendulous hazel catkins or 'lamb's tails' and the fleshy, glossy leaves and developing buds of marsh marigolds around the pond margins. It will however be some weeks before the first of the summer visitors arrive in the garden. Meanwhile the journey into spring will be signposted by a series of firsts, namely the first butterfly or bumblebee, and the first Song Thrush or Blackbird collecting dried grass or moss to build the first nest of the year, a sight to delight the most jaded of hearts.

April

In spite of the rather unsettled weather in March, the garden is exhibiting all the signs of spring. The predominant colour at this time of year is yellow, with daffodils, forsythia, primroses and lesser celandines. I hold a particular affection for these glossy-leaved plants with shiny petals. I leave them unmolested as I weed out the rampant and pungent Bittercress. Dandelions are in full flower under the hedge of greening hawthorn and white flowers of the as yet leafless Blackthorn.

From my sitting-room window I have been watching a Collared Dove fastidiously choosing exactly the right fine twigs to augment the insubstantial platform that is its nest at the top of a cupressus tree. This in time will precariously support two white eggs. An unobtrusive Dunnock is collecting beakfuls of moss to add to its well-concealed nest in a hawthorn hedge. In contrast a female Blackbird is flying into a nearby holly bush conspicuously trailing a bundle of grasses. Another hen Blackbird is building her nest just outside my window in a tangle of Russian vine. These two nests are only a few metres apart and the two cock birds feed on the lawn close to each other under a form of truce. They have ceased to chase each other around the garden. Perhaps there is an invisible line separating their territories.

A Song Thrush is stripping the moss from the paving stones surrounding the large pond. When its beak is full, it flies like a brown bullet to its nest, out of my field of view. By rushing across the room I have just managed to pinpoint the location of its nest from a viewpoint at another window. Observation is the best way to locate birds' nests in the garden. The worst way is to go thrashing through the vegetation, pulling at branches in a frenzy of excitement. This could cause the parent birds to desert their nest, and also make the neighbourhood cat aware of its location. Incidentally the literature states that both male and female Song Thrushes take part in building their nest, but I have observed that only one easily identifiable individual of my pair, gender unknown, is involved in construction.

Two larger birds are currently visitors to the garden. The first is a Carrion Crow, which is building in an oak in an adjacent field. It lands in the tulip tree and proceeds to twist off twigs for its nest. It prefers this material to the much more abundant and far more easily removed pile of twigs on the rubbish heap. The other regular visitor is a Sparrowhawk, the reason for its visits being the numerous small birds congregating around the garden feeding station. In reality its attendance at the bird-table is due to the presence of food, but of the avian and not the cereal variety!

May
The garden is recovering well from the hard frosts suffered over the Easter period and the nesting season is now in full swing. Blue Tits and Great Tits are laying but have not completed their clutches. However the Blackbirds, Song Thrushes, Robins and Dunnocks are tirelessly feeding their rapidly growing families of nestlings.

Some weeks ago I threw out a defunct music-centre but retained the speakers, which were of the old-fashioned type, wooden and box shaped. I removed the internal works and also the front covers, revealing two holes. One of these I covered, leaving the other open, it being of a size suitable for a medium-sized bird. I placed both speakers in suitable locations, one in a tree and the other against the house wall. Within hours a Starling began to carry building material into the former. The other one was not immediately occupied, but some days later a Blackbird began to build its nest on top of it.

Early signs of summer are appearing. Four Swallows were flying over the garden at the end of April and on the same day the plaintive songs of Willow Warblers were heard, along with the song of the Chiffchaff. These two tiny summer migrants are very similar in plumage. They can most easily be distinguished in the field by their songs. In contrast the Garden

Warbler and the Blackcap are less easy to identify by their songs alone. A sighting of the singer quickly determines its identity by the presence or absence of a black cap on the singing male. Both these warblers are grey-brown in colour and are Robin-sized. A Garden Warbler is currently singing in a thicket in the garden.

Drastic action was taken last year to increase the amount of light falling on the large pond by reducing the height of the trees on the south and west sides. The pond is now swarming with brown-speckled frog tadpoles and some jet-black toad tadpoles. The former seem to be a food source for numerous newts. The water is crystal-clear, partly due to the swarms of jerky Daphnia or water-fleas, which are also another useful food-source.

Over the years, Great Crested Newts have established themselves in the pond. A visit to the pond with a torch after dark can reveal several adults, as they emerge into open water from the cover of pondweed to begin their gentle courtship. This protected species is distinguished by its much larger size. It must not be disturbed. Hopefully my small colony will breed successfully and provide offspring to colonise neighbouring garden ponds, building up a viable population of this beautiful and interesting amphibian.

June

June is certainly bursting out all over. I have never seen such an abundance of May, or hawthorn, blossom. The air is full of its scent, whilst the grass verges are awash with a white froth of Hedge Parsley. It is a pity that this time of year passes so quickly.

The hedges and bushes in the garden are heavy with foliage, good cover for a variety of small nesting birds. The field behind my garden is regularly mown. Several Blackbirds and Song Thrushes, seeking earthworms to feed to their growing nestlings, quarter the short grass. Nearly all their first broods failed, predated mostly by crows. Their nests were easily located in the bare branches before the unfolding leaves hid them from view. Broken eggshells, not clean and dry but splattered with yolk, were the evidence of this, proof of their contents having been eaten. The second attempts at nesting have been much more successful, hidden by a thick canopy of foliage. Two pairs of both Song Thrushes and

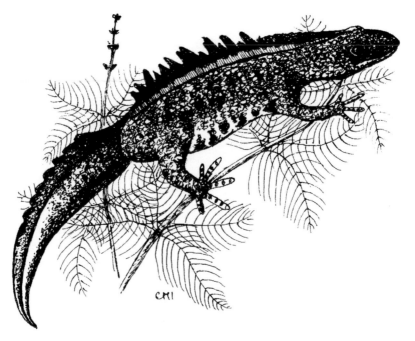

Great Crested Newt

Blackbirds are feeding their young. The nests of the latter species are less than six metres apart. The cocks are surprisingly tolerant of each other, perhaps because they have a large feeding area in the adjacent field.

Three pairs of Blue Tits and one pair of Great Tits are currently nesting in the garden. On either side of the garden shed I had placed a closed-fronted nest-box, offering a choice of position to a pair of house-hunting tits. I was surprised to find that a second pair of Blue Tits began to nest just after a first pair had begun to incubate a clutch of ten eggs. The first box now contains nine young. Eight eggs are being brooded in the second, which is only two metres away from the first! The nest-holes face in opposite directions, so defining different feeding territories. Perhaps it is this fact that permits such tolerance. There appears to be no animosity between the pairs. Whether the garden can produce enough caterpillars to feed the seventeen youngsters and another brood of seven in a box twenty metres away remains to be seen.

At the end of May I caught a fleeting glimpse of a pale-grey and brown bird and two days later there were two of them. The latest of the summer migrants, Spotted Flycatchers, had arrived from Africa. Within three days they had built a tiny cup of a nest between the branch of a climbing rose and the wall of the house. By the end of June two eggs had been laid.

July

What a dismal June we had after a promising start to the month. The cool, wet and windy weather was a near-disaster for some of the nesting garden birds, particularly the Blue Tits. The Great Tit nestlings were the first to fledge, all successfully. The first of the three nests of Blue Tits fledged, but they seemed weak and unable to fly properly, like young thrushes and Blackbirds when they leave their nests. Normally young tits fly freely as soon as they leave the nest and are less likely to be caught by the neighbourhood cat. Only a few of the nestlings of the other two Blue Tit broods survived to fledge. The pathetic corpses of their siblings remained, trampled in the debris at the bottom of the nest-boxes. The inclement weather had perhaps caused a shortage of their staple diet of moth caterpillars. The chicks could have been chilled if left during cool weather while both their parents desperately scavenged for food. Happily the Blackbird and thrush nestlings fledged successfully, sufficient numbers of earthworms being easily obtained from the soft, drenched ground.

Another casualty of the miserable weather was the nest of the Spotted Flycatchers. It became drenched and the eggs were chilled soon after a third egg was laid. This makes it the seventh year in succession that these delightful little birds have tried but failed to raise a brood in the garden. Suitable nest boxes are provided for them, but each year they insist on building during a calm spell in the weather on the house wall, where they are exposed to the prevailing southwesterly wind and rain.

A pair of Wrens has apparently successfully reared young, safe within an impregnable fortress. This consists of an old gatepost that has a rotten interior but with a sound top and surrounding wood. The cock built its leaf-ball of a nest in the cavity and the entrance was a hole just large enough for the tiny owner to come and go. The hen chose this nest from several cock-nests that the male had made, presumably because of its secure situation. It was impossible to examine the nest as the entrance was too small, but after some weeks the parents were seen carrying tiny worms and spiders into the nest hole, the male singing stridently as if confident that the nest was secure from molestation.

August

The cloudy, wet and windy weather continues with an occasional pause for an hour of warm sunshine. One consolation is that I have not had to water the garden once this summer. The soil has remained soft, damp and full of worms, easily accessible to the scavenging Blackbirds and thrushes. In spite of this abundance of meat, these omnivorous birds have been gorging themselves on raspberries and blackcurrants. Some years ago, during a hot dry summer when earthworms were scarce, I decided to leave these soft fruits for the birds to tide them over the drought. In fact, I appreciated avoiding the chore of picking these fiddly fruits. We reserve the rhubarb for ourselves, a food source the birds show no interest in. The berries of the rowan tree are the first of the wild fruits to ripen and are also rapidly being devoured.

For the last few days the garden has been full of round brown balls shooting from bush to bush like jet-propelled tail-less mice or large bumblebees. They turned out to be the numerous progeny of the pair of Wrens that nested in the rotting gatepost. It was impossible to count them but there could have been up to a dozen offspring of this fecund midget of a bird, whose Latin name *Troglodytes troglodytes,* or 'cave-dweller', tells of its preference for nesting in holes and enclosed situations such as hollow gateposts.

For ten days my garden was graced by the presence of two young Great Spotted Woodpeckers, flying around the garden with a loud *'tchich'* call. These welcome visitors are somewhat larger than a Song Thrush, with black and white plumage and red crowns. They clung to the bird-table post and then hung on the tit-feeders, but had difficulty feeding due to their large chisel-like bills. Currently this species of woodpecker is quite common in our area, in contrast to its larger cousin the Green Woodpecker, which seems to have all but deserted us.

September

This has been the worst summer I can ever remember, dull, damp and windy. It is only in the last few days that the weather has brightened a little and butterflies have again begun to visit the garden. I have planted two buddleias in the sunniest part of the garden and within minutes several Peacocks, two Red Admirals, and a single Small Tortoiseshell butterfly were nectaring on the glistening flowers. In order to attract swarms of butterflies, buddleias should be planted in a dry and sunny position and the bushes pruned regularly to produce fresh growth and flowers. Two other herbaceous plants are a must for attracting butterflies into the wildlife garden in late summer and early autumn, the ice-plant, *Sedum spectabile,* and Michaelmas daisy. The buds of both of these butterfly favourites are just beginning to open.

Wasps seem particularly abundant at the moment. A neighbour has a nest close to his house. Each of the fallen apples, mutilated by the beaks of hungry Blackbirds, has a feeding cluster of these insects. Neighbours have spoken of the lethargic state of these normally active insects. I have been watching them swarming around a willow tree. An individual will alight on a leaf and walk around its perimeter seemingly feeding on something on the surface. It cannot be honeydew as no aphids are present but possibly some exudation from the leaf itself.

For the last few years I have noticed that the leaves of the shady garden plant, Solomon's Seal, have been reduced to a ragged midrib. Neighbouring gardeners have suffered the same infestation. The culprit is the larva of a sawfly that arrived about a century ago and has since spread over most of the country. They have completely devoured the leaf tissue between the veins. Although at this time of the year all that remains are leaf skeletons, the plants are never completely killed. The sawfly larva has at least six pairs of stumpy legs, while the moth or butterfly caterpillar has never more than five.

After a period of complete absence of bird song, the garden Robins have begun their plaintive autumn lament, heralding the end of summer, for once this year not regretted. The Swifts have long departed and in the weeks to come the other summer visitors will have left the wildlife garden as we drift into autumn and perhaps better weather.

October

After a miserable summer, the weather during the second half of September has been a godsend to the gardener! Day after day of dry and usually sunny weather has enabled the backbreaking work of pruning, digging and branch-cutting to take place. Wildlife gardening requires constant management and is not an excuse to let nature take her course. I have spent most of this period lowering the height of the silver birch and cupressus trees on the south side of the garden, as well as cutting down the shrubs to manageable dimensions. Buddleia bushes, which have been overgrown by more vigorous shrubs, have been rediscovered. I will make certain that they will be free to flower and attract more butterflies next summer.

Light in a garden is always at a premium and during this gloomy summer the ponds in particular have suffered from a deficit of this life-sustaining commodity. I have removed large quantities of floating water-plants such as *Elodea* to allow light to penetrate to the pond bottom. This will increase the water temperature and so encourage the growth of water-lilies. Growing with the *Elodea* were masses of a plant that I have only recently become aware of, *Crassula helmsii*, or New Zealand pigmyweed. It is rampant and invasive but can easily be removed by the handful. However it is useful in providing cover, and as a base for egg laying for both fish and newts. It is also a means for removing excess nutrients from the pond water and so reducing the chance of a pea-green soup of algae.

When one removes excess vegetation from the pond, one must be careful not to inadvertently remove legitimate inhabitants, such as young newts and water-beetle larvae. Place the weeds in a suitable receptacle such as an inverted dustbin lid, leave for some time, then carefully search for any hidden minibeasts. They can then be gently returned to the pond, before placing the vegetation on the compost heap.

There has been little activity around the bird-table of late, perhaps due to the abundance of food available in the fields and hedgerows at this time of year. As autumn progresses our local bird-life will become more dependent on food we supply to them in our gardens. Some anxiety has recently been expressed concerning the spread of disease at garden feeding-stations where supplementary food, particularly peanuts, is provided. In order to reduce the chance of disease, hanging feeders should be moved frequently around a number of sites. Droppings have less chance to accumulate beneath, and the weather breaks them down into the grass. Periodically the bird table should be cleaned with warm water and disinfectant.

November

At the beginning of October, a Collared Dove was seen fastidiously choosing fine twigs and carrying them to a horizontal branch ten feet up in a Scots pine. It appeared that the same bird did the collecting while its mate arranged the material into a flat flimsy nest. This structure looked too insubstantial to withstand all but the calmest of weather, yet during the following weeks it has withstood the onslaught of gale-force winds and torrential rain. The constant presence of the sitting bird may have anchored the frail nest, with its pair of white eggs, to the level branch, and to date it has survived. In an adjacent tall cupressus tree a Woodpigeon is also sitting on its two eggs, though in a much more sheltered situation. These two species of related vegetarians often nest at a time of year when most other birds are preparing for winter. The Woodpigeons are feeding from a carpet of mast fallen from the nearby beech tree. This food source appears to be too bulky for the Collared Doves. They prefer the chicken feed I place on the bird-table.

The season of leaf fall is with us and so I have once again covered the ponds with netting to prevent falling leaves from blowing into the water and causing pollution. This however creates a problem for frogs. They wish to enter the water in order to hibernate in the mud at the bottom. One agile amphibian was seen bouncing on the netting like a sumo wrestler on a trampoline, while another was trying to squeeze under the edge like a competitor in an obstacle race. An answer to this problem is to roll back some of the netting from the side of the pond furthest away from the trees and drifting leaves. The ubiquitous garden ornaments such as stone frogs and gnomes can anchor the other edges of the nets. Birds actually find the netting useful as a means of access to the ponds, which are normally too deep for them for bathing.

This autumn I looked everywhere in the surrounding countryside for mushrooms but to no avail. Yet in my garden I found a large clump of fungi. They looked, smelled and peeled like mushrooms. I risked eating a small quantity of the fried material with no terminal outcome or even discomfort, for they were indeed mushrooms. However my advice is to pick mushrooms in a supermarket unless one is an expert!

The leaves of polyanthus are like sheets of Nottingham lace thanks to the activities of swarms of slugs and snails this wet season. I resisted the impulse to put slug-pellets down as this could contribute to the demise of our resident Song Thrushes. In many parts of the country Song Thrushes are known to be declining.

December

November is arguably the most forgettable time of the year and we are always relieved when this gloomy damp month is behind us. Its sheer dreariness however can have pleasant interludes, such as when chattering flocks of Fieldfares descend like aerial pirates onto the high hawthorn hedge to strip the branches bare of their harvest of haws. Each bird defends a feeding zone from its garrulous neighbours. As yet their smaller and less vocal cousins, the Redwings, have yet to visit the garden this season.

On several occasions in the past month, during periods of mild weather, one and sometimes two Red Admirals were seen nectaring on the abundant ivy flowers. Hopefully this usually migratory butterfly will hibernate, successfully survive the winter, and possibly breed next year.

The young Collared Doves have left their nest and are sitting tightly together like two lovebirds on a birch branch while their parents forage on the ground for tiny seeds. They have been in full view for two weeks, literally a sitting target for the resident Sparrowhawk. Perhaps they have been overlooked because of their lack of movement and the fact that their dove-grey plumage blends in with the colour of the birch bark. They are exact replicas of their parents except for their lack of a collar.

Though some Blue Tits are visiting the nut-feeders, the winter feeding frenzy on the bird-table has yet to begin. There must be enough insects and berries in the surrounding hedgerows to satisfy their appetites, but any bread on the table disappears in one gulp if a resident of the neighbouring rookery honours us with a flying visit.

Often in winter a Grey Wagtail visits the garden and this year has been no exception. This graceful yellow and blue-grey bird is normally found near water, usually in hilly areas, but outside the breeding season it sometimes searches for insects around garden ponds. On this occasion it landed on the damp flat roof of the house, perhaps thinking it was part of a flooded meadow and a possible source of food. It quickly realised its mistake and flew to the nearby ponds.

Pedunculate Oak

January

The footnote to last month's saga of the Collared Dove twins is, I'm afraid, a sad one, as some days later a scattering of dove-grey feathers was found close to their perch. I have not seen either of the youngsters since. I'm nearly certain that the agent of their demise was the local Sparrowhawk. As if to advertise its presence, a male Sparrowhawk, hardly larger than a Mistle Thrush, for which I initially mistook it, was seen bathing in the large pond. It stood on the net draped over the surface to collect fallen leaves. It was identifiable as a male by its small size and finely barred reddish-yellow breast.

The Collared Doves have suffered double trouble. As well as losing their offspring, their nesting tree, a large and sturdy Scots pine, has been blown over at an angle of 25 degrees to the vertical, propped up by two large adjacent cypresses.

February

It is important that the bird table is secure from the attention of predators, but also that it can be clearly and comfortably seen from a suitable window, particularly in the winter time. There was a slack period after Christmas, when there appeared to be a surfeit of food in the hedgerows and fields, but lately there has been an invasion of tits and finches to the garden feeding-stations. When I scatter handfuls of mixed wild bird food on the bird-table I notice that the sunflower seeds are eaten first, followed by the smaller grains, leaving the larger cereals to be cleaned up during occasional visits by Woodpigeons and Rooks. Flocks of Blue, Great and Coal Tits visit the nut-feeder, along with an increasing numbers of birds which normally feed on the ground, such as Robins and Chaffinches.

Two mornings ago I watched with interest the frenetic feeding of a tiny grey bird with a pale yellow crown. It was a Goldcrest, our smallest bird. It flew rapidly from one branch of an apple tree to another, diligently searching crevices in the bark for its prey of minute flies or spiders. One would think that the nutritional value of its meagre food sources would not compensate for the energy output of its hyperactive hunting. The resident pair of Collared Doves were recently observed collecting fine twigs once again. Nest building had begun in a tall cupressus tree adjacent to a Scots pine. These small immigrant pigeons appear to nest all the year round.

March

For the first time this winter, two female Siskins have been feeding regularly, hanging upside-down on the nut-feeders. In the countryside these small finches, similar to diminutive Greenfinches, hang upside-down whilst feeding from the tips of birch and alder branches. Parties of up to six of these delightful little seedeaters have recently visited neighbours' bird-tables.

Many of the apples stored in the garage have become shrunken and wizened. The decaying ones have been placed in the compost bin, but some of the sound ones I have placed in a pile under the bird-table, to the

Goldcrest

delight of the Blackbirds, which are feasting on them. A considerable number of the stored apples have again been attacked by Long-tailed Field-mice over the winter. I discovered that all the cheese, which had been placed as bait in a live-trap, had been eaten, but the trip wire had not triggered the trapdoor. It had stuck! Copious quantities of a lubricant got the mechanism working smoothly, and subsequently on six consecutive mornings the trap contained a brown, bright-eyed rodent. These charming visitors were temporarily housed in a large empty fish-tank with food, water and bedding, prior to being released away from the house. The strong smell of the lubricant was no deterrent to these inquisitive creatures. Perhaps the pungent aroma masked the scent of humans.

Blackbirds and Song Thrushes are chasing each other around the garden as they establish nesting territories. The tangle of Russian vine outside the living room window is being investigated as a prospective nest-site by a hen Blackbird. Most of the birds are in full song and the tits are feverishly examining the nest-boxes, tapping away at the entrance holes.

Frogs have been active for some time now after hibernation in the mud at the bottom of the ponds. While carefully removing the nets with their coating of leaves from the ponds I was nearly hit by the resident Sparrowhawk as it dived over the boundary hedge. On clearing some of the excess Canadian waterweed *(Elodea)* I came across several adult Common and Palmate Newts that may have entered the water from the rockery. In addition there were a number of tiny immature newts. They must have hibernated at a very early stage in their development.

April

At breakfast time on 3rd March I witnessed a protracted and vicious fight between two rivals. The protagonists were not cats or dogs but cock Blackbirds. They were fighting in the vicinity of the bird-table where they had been feeding on the remains of last year's apples, in the company of five hen Blackbirds. They attacked each other with beak and claw; the claws were used to lock the opponent to the ground, while the beak stabbed like a sword. Not to be outdone, two of the females initiated a tussle between themselves while another, perhaps the mate of one of the protagonists, briefly intervened in the males' fight. I have witnessed several similar combats. They may be a result of a high density of breeding pairs living in close proximity with neighbours. There is a shortage of suitable nesting habitat adjoining a large feeding area. I am also fortunate in having two pairs of Song Thrushes nesting in the garden. Conflict between these rivals is restricted to posing. They face each other like statues until one gives way, chased off by its rival, accompanied by loud alarm calls.

As in every community, housing development is taking place in our village. This does not necessarily bode ill for the local wildlife, as a piece of sterile field may be turned into a mosaic of lawns, bushes, creepers and ponds, as well as bricks and mortar. Hopefully the new occupants will encourage wildlife by providing bird-food in winter and flowers in summer for butterflies and bees. The downside is the increase in the number of cats and the possible use of pesticides and herbicides.

The frogs spawned late this year, not until 13th March, and they avoided the large pond. They entered all the ponds initially but the loudest concentration of croaks seemed to attract individuals from smaller groups: a kind of slimy snowball effect. Then, when one pair lays, it precipitates a frenzy of spawning. I distributed some spawn into the large pond but avoided placing any in the smallest pond, where to my surprise coils of toad-spawn had been laid. The toads may have used this pond because some twigs were tangled in the waterweed, making a better anchor to wrap strings of spawn around. I am a little concerned that the spawn may be infertile, as I have not heard the piping call of a male toad.

Several species of birds are nest building, including Blackbirds, Collared Doves and Song Thrushes. The air is full of bird-song at dusk. One song I did not recognise initially was that of a Siskin. I confirmed its identity by observing the songster. It would be nice to have these delightful little finches nesting in our gardens.

May

April has ended like it began with warm and sunny weather. Unfortunately the middle portion of the sandwich has been cold and wintry, but this has not affected the successful nesting of the garden birds. Last month's conflict between two pairs of Song Thrushes has been resolved. One pair is still feeding young, whilst the brood from the other nest has successfully fledged. The young were brooded for some days after hatching by the hen, but the cock, instead of continuously food-gathering, had time to sing for quite protracted periods. This was perhaps an indication of an abundance of prey, particularly earthworms, obtained easily from the moist soil and short grass of the adjoining field.

In a Sitka spruce a Woodpigeon clattered onto its nest, losing a loose feather as it did so. A House Sparrow caught the feather in mid-air and was flying with it to its nest in the ivy. A Starling bullied the sparrow into releasing the feather, which it caught and carried to its own nest where it had five raucous young. The House Sparrow has five granite-patterned eggs in an untidy weaverbird-type nest stuffed into the ivy on the south-facing wall of my bungalow. A metre away another sparrow built, but has since deserted, perhaps due to incessant quarrels between the two pairs.

In the clematis opposite the front door a cock Wren has built a nest, a smaller tidier version of the House Sparrow's nest. This as yet has no lining so it is still a 'cock nest', not yet accepted by the hen for laying her eggs in. A Robin is sitting on its clutch of six eggs, situated in a vulnerable position on the ground between a garden tub and the house wall. The eggs are near to hatching but as yet have been overlooked by prowling cats.

A Chaffinch has built a beautiful cup-shaped nest of moss and lichen, well camouflaged in a fork of the lichen-covered apple tree. Both the Blue Tits and Great Tits have laid in their nest-boxes, and the Collared

Doves and Woodpigeons are brooding their couplets of shiny white eggs. Altogether the nesting season is progressing satisfactorily.

The pond is a hive of activity. Now that the frogs and toads have spawned, it's the time of the newts and all three species are breeding. It is exciting to creep out after dark and shine a powerful torch into the water to watch the Great Crested Newts courting, the males fanning the females with their bluish-white striped tails. Hopefully they will lay numerous eggs, and so will produce plenty of young of this protected species. Unfortunately the future of these particular newtlets may be threatened by the presence of a Golden Orfe, an ornamental fish that has mysteriously transferred itself from the ornamental fishpond to the amphibian pond. The speed and agility of this torpedo-shaped fish make it difficult to net in the plant-clogged water. It is a threat to the young amphibians and I wish the Golden Orfe would 'push orf'!

June

As we move into June four Great Tit nestlings have left their nest-box and the two broods of Blue Tits are ready for fledging. The first pair of Blue Tits to nest produced a clutch of ten eggs, of which eight hatched. Two of these nestlings were runts. Whether they were late hatching or late developers I do not know, as being away for several days I did not follow their development. One soon died but its retarded sibling survived, doubling its weight. Sadly however it succumbed after several days. Perhaps resources were limited and it could not compete for food with six healthy brothers and sisters. In the nest sibling rivalry can be very cruel! Of the other clutch of eight Blue Tit eggs, six nestlings have also survived to the fledgling stage. Consistently over the years two pairs of Blue Tits and one pair of Great Tits have nested in the garden. This ratio perhaps reflects the national populations of these common garden birds. I have also noted that without exception both the clutch and fledgling sizes of the Blue Tits is always higher than that of the Great Tits.

Three broods of Blackbirds and two of Song Thrushes have successfully fledged. It always surprises me that quite conspicuous birds can nest unobserved right under one's nose. A brood of five Blackbird chicks was near to fledging before the nest was found in clematis three metres from my front door. Another pair built a nest on top of a nest-box

Wren

that I regularly inspected. I had failed to notice its presence! Two pairs of Blackbirds are nesting only eight metres apart, indicative of a high density of this songbird thanks to a more than adequate food supply.

While gazing up into a cupressus tree to locate the nest of a Woodpigeon, I found myself looking at a pair of dark eyes in a grey-brown face. They were gazing at me from a small bundle of twigs in the fork of a branch; it was a Collared Dove, nesting within a few feet of its larger cousin. For some days it appeared to brood continuously what I thought were eggs or small young. On inspecting the nest I discovered that the 'brood' consisted of a solitary and nearly full-grown squab. Having only one beak to feed, the parents could enjoy the luxury of restful brooding.

I was recently pleased to observe several specimens of the Large Red Damselfly flitting over the pond and resting on nearby vegetation. These small slender dragonflies emerge in early summer. The establishment of a colony of these colourful carnivorous insects increases the biodiversity of the wildlife garden.

July

Another 'flaming June' has passed! There have been some sunny spells but the month has been characterised by heavy thundery showers, the consolation being no requirement to water the garden or top up the ponds.

The Golden Orfe, which managed to relocate itself from the ornamental fishpond to the wildlife pond, still remains free, a threat to the pond's inhabitants. It taunts me by lying in full view just under the surface in an open part of the pond like a pale symmetrical carrot. Whenever I try, net in hand, to creep up and capture it, it disappears without trace into the vegetation. Orfe are swift and agile, unlike clumsy lethargic goldfish. I tried trapping it by placing nets below floating bait but all to no avail. In desperation I even went to the extreme of trying to catch it on a worm-baited hook. It deftly removed the worm from the hook without being snagged. On another occasion, on seeing the float bob under, I quickly pulled in the line only to find a twisting Great Crested Newt, its jaws locked on the worm. I placed the indignant amphibian back in the pond and tried again. A short time later the worm was surrounded by a rugby scrum of about a dozen newts, the two 'prop-forwards' being two Great Crested Newts. On withdrawing the worm I found two Smooth Newts locked onto it with their tiny teeth. I quickly released them, unharmed, back into the water and conceded that the orfe had won.

I must report a piece of classic good news / bad news. On 10th June I observed two Spotted Flycatchers, one feeding the other, obviously a pair! The following day, to my surprise, I found a flycatchers' nest less than a metre away from my front door, containing four eggs. It had been completely overlooked. To avoid disturbing the sitting bird we had to alter our lifestyle, including entering and leaving the house by the garage, and in spite of some unavoidable interruptions all four eggs hatched on 24th June. The behaviour of the birds I had watched on 10th June was not compatible with incubating a clutch of eggs. My prognosis was proved when I found another flycatchers' nest. There was a second pair of flycatchers nesting in the garden! The second nest was built on a climbing-rose trellis on the south wall of the house. The second pair completed a clutch of four eggs on 27th June. However my euphoria evaporated when on 28th June the nest at the front door was found to be tipped up and empty, probably the result of Magpie or Crow predation. Happily the second pair is still brooding, in spite of the nest's exposure to the heavy showers of the last few days. If this nest survives it will be the first such success in the garden, but I will not count my flycatchers until they fledge.

August

Firstly, a piece of good news! Three of the Spotted Flycatchers' eggs in the nest on the rose trellis hatched on 9th July. I was relieved to see two parents feeding the youngsters. I had been worried when, on two occasions, piles of feathers were found on the lawn looking suspiciously like flycatcher feathers, the remains of cat kills. Perhaps the casualties were the flycatchers that were unsuccessful in their breeding attempt near the front porch. The youngsters fledged on 23rd July, fourteen days after hatching. After many years of failure a pair of these delightful little birds has finally succeeded in rearing a brood, in spite of Crows, cats, Magpies and thundery downpours. It was thrilling to see a young bird sitting on our living-room windowsill while its hovering parent brought it fly after fly.

It has been a good nesting season for the garden songbirds. Half a dozen broods each of thrushes and Blackbirds have successfully fledged. There have also been several nests of Collared Doves and Woodpigeons. One Woodpigeon clutch of two white eggs was predated, perhaps by a passing Crow. However the parents were not deterred and laid two more eggs in the same nest, optimism indeed! A foolish action, I thought, but I was proved wrong when the eggs hatched, and after a couple of weeks of being fed on pigeon's milk the young left the nest. Pigeon's milk is not really milk, but a secretion produced by pigeons with which they feed their chicks. Both the male and the female start to produce it just before their chicks hatch. These overweight youngsters did not fly away at once but spent several days perching on branches in the vicinity of the nest, being fed by their industrious parents.

A pest that seems to have invaded many gardens recently is the wasp, which often takes up residence in bird-boxes. There are two wasps' nests in my garden. One has been built in an open-fronted nest-box. It seems a pity to destroy the beautiful structure, papery and pear-shaped, built so laboriously over the last few months. Unfortunately at this time of year the wasps have changed from beneficial insect-eating gardeners' friends to fruit-devouring pests, and at times a painful nuisance.

The recent hot weather has produced an algal bloom in the ornamental fishpond, causing some distress to the inhabitants, and necessitating a complete clean-out and change of water. On lifting the rigid plastic pond from its bed in order to decant the remaining pool of smelly water, I was excited to discover a tangle of newts, four of which were Great Crested Newts, two fully grown. They had hidden themselves in a hollow below the lip of the edge of the pond. It often appears as if newts disappear into thin air when leaving the ponds, but like toads they secrete themselves into holes. In addition to this discovery I was pleased to find several Great Crested Newt tadpoles, the first time I have had evidence of this protected amphibian breeding in my garden.

September

For the last week or two plaintive sounds have been heard in the garden. These are the autumn songs of the resident Robins, indicative of the approach of the end of summer and the inevitable advance of autumn with its dew, mists and fruits. Blackberries have ripened in the hedges, swollen by the recent rains and the panicles of elderberries droop under the weight of their black fruit. Now is the time to make homemade wine from the harvest of garden and hedgerow fruits.

Two events of note took place recently. One had a happy ending, one unfortunately not! One evening a very young rabbit ran straight past me, dived into the large pond and swam the full length but could not get out. It then froze at the edge as if mesmerised by a hunting Stoat. It allowed me to lift it out, a wet limp ball. After a minute or so it awoke from its state of shock and loped off into the bushes. Only two mornings later I was sad to find in the pond the body of a very young Hedgehog. It had obviously fallen in, been unable to clamber out and had died from

Spotted Flycatcher

drowning or hypothermia. I had planted one edge of the pond with marginals to facilitate the entrance and exit of amphibians but obviously young inexperienced mammals panic, like young humans, and the hedgehog didn't make use of this lifeline. I must make better provision for the escape of such victims. Garden ponds can be a lethal danger for young garden mammals as well as for very young humans.

I have previously mentioned the invasive nature of a recently introduced water plant, *Crassula helmsii,* or New Zealand pigmyweed. Initially I was not perturbed when it colonised my ponds at a prodigious rate, as it provided cover and a spawning medium for newts. By frequently removing clumps I was indirectly lowering the mineral salt concentration of the pond-water and so reducing the possibility of an algal bloom. However I observed that all the *Elodea* – Canadian waterweed – had disappeared and I wondered if it had been suffocated by the *Crassula*. I removed all of this plant and thanks to the generosity of friends restocked the ponds with *Elodea*. One plants this oxygenator by arranging half-a-dozen shoots in a sheaf, tying it to a stone and sinking the clump to the bottom, where it will root. The growing tips will push towards the surface. After several weeks the *Elodea* has increased considerably and formed several large healthy clumps, improving the oxygen content of the water. The fish in the ornamental pond no longer gasp at the surface during periods of hot weather.

October

Many indicators in the wildlife garden mark the inexorable advance of autumn. Most of the House Martins and Swallows have left for the south but a few stragglers have been seen about the village in the last few days, perhaps reluctant to leave because of the mild Indian summer weather. A Chiffchaff has been heard after a silence of a couple of months. It is hidden amongst the leaves, which are slowly changing to red and gold in the increasingly clammy and chilly air.

Some days ago I was called to a neighbour's garden to witness the quite spectacular sight of up to thirty Red Admiral butterflies feeding on a pile of fruit at the foot of a pear tree. These beautiful black, red and white insects flapping and gliding over the windfalls gave quite an exotic touch to the scene. It will be interesting to see whether any of these mainly migrant butterflies will over-winter.

The garden has been affected by three 'plagues' this late summer and early autumn. Firstly there have been swarms of daddy-long-legs or 'ginnie-spinners'. They have been particularly annoying at night, flying into the house through any open lighted windows, and also clogging up the moth-trap. The larvae of these crane flies, to use their Sunday name, are the so-called 'leather-jackets', so destructive of grassland. They are a main component of the diet of Starlings, which are often to be seen stabbing away on lawns in their quest for this pest.

I have never before seen such a harvest of birch seeds as this year. They will be welcomed by restless flocks of small finches, such as Redpolls, feeding frenetically on the topmost branches. Seeds cover the ground and the car like a light fall of snow and are only a minor nuisance, unlike the third plague. The house has been invaded by Stable-flies. Their number may be higher because of the proximity of horses and their straw bedding. Others in the village also report large numbers of these silent biters. They resemble small Houseflies, but cruise silently at ankle height. One only becomes aware of their presence when experiencing a sharp

93

pain in the foot or lower leg. A slap is useless, a swipe with a folded newspaper is much more effective.

November
The clocks have gone back one hour and we have entered the dark time of the year. The only consolation is that as we move relentlessly deeper into the winter gloom each day takes us closer to the rebirth of a new year. On the bright side is the arrival of flocks of chattering Fieldfares from Scandinavia. Along with their smaller cousins the Redwings, these handsome grey thrushes festoon the hedges where they feed on the harvest of hips and haws. Unfortunately some of the nearby field hedges have been cut early this autumn, reducing the supply of ripened berries. This makes it more imperative for us gardeners to supply an alternative food supply in the form of hedgerow fruits, including elder and hawthorn.

It is now the bonfire season but don't burn all the products of hedge trimming and tree-pruning. Pile some in a secluded corner of the garden to provide shelter for small garden residents such as ladybirds and bumblebees as well as for hibernating Hedgehogs. In spring it will give cover for early-nesting Blackbirds, Robins and Wrens, particularly before the unfolding leaves provide protection.

I only found a few mushrooms this year in the usual places I visit, but was pleased to find several huge specimens growing below my high privet hedge. This event has occurred for the last few years without fail. This is now the fungus season and one can come across crouched groups of fungal forayers in secluded situations endeavouring to increase their knowledge of the several thousand species of these organisms found in Britain. It would be fascinating to count the number of varieties found in one's own garden.

Recently I was given the opportunity of comparing the largest and one of the smallest hopping birds. A Mistle Thrush, considerably larger than our more familiar Song Thrush, was feeding on worms on the lawn, completely dwarfing a spider-hunting Wren. While watching this avian David and Goliath my gaze was drawn to a beautiful yellow and grey-blue bird with bobbing tail balancing on the strands of netting placed over the pond. It was the Grey Wagtail, more usually seen in summer by fast-moving water. It was catching and eating pondskaters. It would not have been able to do this but for the support of the netting placed over the pond to prevent wind-blown leaves from entering the water. These pond skaters have waxed fat on food, particularly the dried cat food, with which I have been feeding the fish. When a pellet falls on the surface a scrum of skaters surround it, thinking it is a drowning fly. As the crumb becomes soggy and soft, tiny pieces break off and the insects appear to feed on these. However there is a mystery that I have not as yet solved. Some of the floating pellets vibrate like a float above bitten bait on a fishing line. I have still to identify the diminutive denizens responsible for this effect: another of the interesting problems to solve in the wildlife garden.

December

A few days ago a thrush-sized bird, black-and-white with a red crown, visited. It hung on the tit-feeder, stabbing frenetically through the wire mesh to get at the peanuts inside. This welcome visitor was of course a Great Spotted Woodpecker, of the three British woodpeckers by far the one most frequently seen in our area. Its presence dissuaded the more usual customers from attending, except for a pair of Collared Doves feeding on the mixed grain on the bird-table. After the woodpecker departed the feeder again became festooned with Blue Tits until a male Sparrowhawk, hardly bigger than a Blackbird, appeared on the scene. It targeted one unfortunate tit, which, instead of diving for cover, flew dizzily round and round the bird-table with the raptor in close pursuit. Amazingly it managed to escape, and because nature has a short memory the feeder was soon covered again with its crop of tits.

Swallows and flycatchers migrate south for the winter because at this time of year there are few flying insects on which they feed. There are however several species of moth about. The names of some of them reflect the season when they are seen, such as the November, the December and the Winter Moths. These insects can be seen fluttering in the car headlights on all but the coldest nights.

The short dull days are brightened by the celandine-yellow of the winter jasmine, and the air is full of the scent of winter-sweet. A pair of Collared Doves is feeding two young in a cupressus. Life goes on as we enter the new millennium in the wildlife garden.

2000

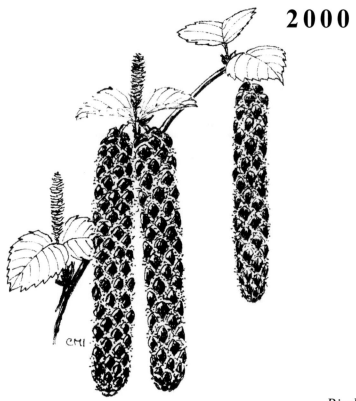

Birch

January

This is the third year running when we have experienced violent storms towards the end of December. Last year it was on Boxing Day that a severe gust of wind pushed my not-insubstantial Scots pine over to an angle of twenty-five degrees. It was supported by two neighbouring cupressus, large and sturdy trees. After some deliberation we considered that it seemed stable enough to leave in that position. During most of last year it remained firmly lodged and safe. Our confidence was reinforced when a pair of Collared Doves risked their pair of fragile eggs on a sloping platform of a nest. However on Christmas Eve our optimism was shattered when a severe gale completely uprooted the tree and made an adjoining cupressus unstable. A friend with a chain saw cut down the trees, rendering them no longer a threat to life and property. The sections of trunk have been made into a heap where hopefully in time they will become home for various small garden residents. The branches I have piled against the hedge to provide shelter for voles, shrews and Hedgehogs.

A female Sparrowhawk settled in the high hawthorn hedge immediately outside my study window. I watched it for some time, expecting it to fly away, but it seemed at ease and began to preen itself. The clamour of the small birds began to fade and their behaviour became routine. It was as if they knew that the hawk was of no threat, as it was not hunting, just as wildebeest ignore a resting lion. The Sparrowhawk then spread the feathers of its wings and tail as if enjoying the gentle warmth of the winter sunshine. It remained in that position for forty minutes, long enough for me to erect a tripod, attach to it my camera and long lens and take many photographs of the hawk in its various poses.

A visit more threatening to the resident garden birds was that made by a male Sparrowhawk. It perched on the pitched roof of the bird-table for half a minute as if daring any small bird to come and feed. These beautiful little raptors visit the garden on an almost daily basis and I feel that their presence is indicative of a large, healthy garden bird population and should be welcomed.

A tiny grey, white and brown bird with a black cap and bib has visited the garden on several occasions recently, sometimes with its mate. It is a Marsh Tit, which is something like a Coal Tit but without the white flash on its nape. As it is a bird new to the garden I shall call it my Millennium Bird.

February

The days are getting longer and even though we are still in the middle of winter there are already signs of spring. A Song Thrush emitted a short burst of song during a mild sunny period in mid January. On 24th January, which was a beautiful spring-like day, the same bird sang for a protracted period. This vocal activity ceased when the cold, wet and windy weather returned.

The snowdrops are in full flower, and the green spears of the daffodil

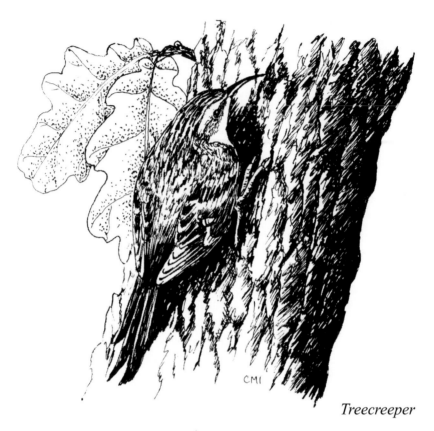

Treecreeper

leaves rise imperceptibly, phoenix-like, from the cold wet earth as if in anticipation of better weather to come. The usual motley crew of finches and tits are feeding at the bird-table but as yet I have not seen a Siskin. This appears to be repeating the pattern of last year when only one of these tiny finches visited the nut-feeders.

Yesterday I saw a small grey mouse-like bird spiralling up one of the apple trees, diligently searching for tiny insects and spiders hidden in crevices in its bark. The Treecreeper is a regular visitor to the garden, but as yet it has not nested, due to an absence of suitable nesting-sites. They like to nest in deep fissures in tree-trunks. I have tried to encourage Treecreepers to nest by placing special boxes, wedge-shaped with an entrance hole flush with the trunk, on the sides of trees.

March

I caught my first moth of the year in the moth-trap on 5th February. This insect is appropriately called the Early Moth. It was a male. Only the males fly, the females being all-but-wingless, a characteristic also shown by some other female moths abroad during the winter season. Perhaps it is an adaptation to insure that the female, with its valuable cargo of eggs, is not blown away in the winter storms.

On 12th February I first heard the cascading song of the Chaffinch. For some weeks the 'twice-over' chant of the Song Thrush has been heard, as well as its harsh scolding chatter, as several pairs mark out the perimeters of their nesting territories. As yet I have not heard the mellow fluting notes of the Blackbird, more likely to be heard on warmer spring days.

On the same day a neighbour came to the door to announce that a large brownish bird was lying outside her front porch. The object of her concern turned out to be a female Sparrowhawk. I recognised this bird as being the same one I had photographed some weeks ago through my study window, identified by a distinctive pattern of white and brown on its wing-coverts. It must have struck the glass of the porch window, presumably when chasing its quarry. It remained long enough to enable me to take some more photographs of it, before flapping away, appearing not to have suffered any permanent damage.

My conscience has been troubling me since last summer when I introduced, for aesthetic reasons, some ornamental fish into the large pond. Until then it had been solely the residence of several amphibian species. Fish can have a particularly deleterious effect on newts, not least by eating their young. Over the winter I had toyed with the idea of digging another large pond specifically for amphibians, but for reasons of logistics and lethargy I decided against it. Then I had a brainwave! When we first moved to our present house I had dug a pond that over the years had slowly changed into a swamp, the main agent of this succession being the invasive flag-iris. I decided to remove this vigorous marginal and on digging out the matted clumps I disturbed clusters of indignant frogs rudely awakened from hibernation. I found the original liner to be cracked and torn and so I bought a new one. The following morning in the puddle that had formed at the deep end of the pond there was a scrum of frogs. I

99

carefully removed them before beginning to place the new liner on top of the old. I placed the liner over the excavation and made it taught like a drum skin by anchoring it around the edges with stones, then slowly added water with a hosepipe. The liner sank slowly down under the weight of the water until it settled into the contours of the excavation of the 'old' pond. When the pond was filled, *Elodea* and other aquatic plants were placed in the water and flat stones allowed to sink onto the clumps, so anchoring them to the pond bottom. After a few days, and during a spell of wet and mild weather, about thirty frogs could be seen to have entered the 'new' pond. Hopefully in the days to come toads and newts will follow them into this fish-free environment.

I have marked off an area of the lawn adjacent to the ponds that will remain uncut this spring, so allowing plants such as cuckooflower to flower where they have been suppressed for years by constant mowing. As well as their mauve flowers providing colour in the garden, their succulent leaves provide fodder for the caterpillars of the Orange-tip butterfly.

April

It is typical of the capricious British weather that, at the end of a mild winter and after the spring equinox has passed, the weather gets colder. However in spite of keen easterly winds and frosty nights, the nesting season is in full swing. The garden Blackbirds and Song Thrushes have completed building their nests and a Collared Dove is sitting on its two eggs in the cupressus, near my newly renovated pond. A Robin has half-completed its nest of dry brown beech leaves just under the sill of the kitchen window, frustratingly just out of sight. A pair of Starlings has taken possession of a larger closed-fronted nest-box outside the dining-room window. On several occasions we have been entertained by the resident pair's antics when challenged for possession of the box by another pair of Starlings. However possession is nine tenths of the law and the original occupants have kept control, establishing their claim by vigorous pecking of the branches close to the box. Conflict has also arisen between pairs of both Song Thrushes and Robins. The Robins particularly displayed aggression with jerky posturing and vicious pecking, completely contrary to the traditional sentimental thoughts about 'Robin

Siskin

Redbreast'. Two pairs of Blackbirds seem to have settled their differences, though the conflict may have resulted in the demise of an immaculate cock Blackbird I picked up on the lawn.

The frogs have finished spawning and most have left the water. Interestingly, the large pond into which I introduced ornamental fish last summer contains no spawn at all. However the pond which I cleaned out and relined, and which contains no fish, is full of spawn. I wonder whether the presence of a number of fish, some of which are quite large, discourages frogs from spawning, especially when there is a fish-free pond nearby.

More birds are coming to the bird-table for food. Early spring is a lean time for them, as nearly all the seeds and fruits, left over from the autumn, have been eaten. So it is imperative not to cease feeding the garden birds at this time. The tit-feeders are festooned with several species of tits and finches, including up to three Siskins. Some of these tiny green finches always visit in early spring.

I recently was excited to see a pair of Long-tailed Tits flitting around the garden. One of these tiny birds fluttered up against the kitchen window where it was picking up small pieces of lichen from the top of the frame. They are obviously nesting in the area, hopefully in my garden.

We all know about the Robin which waits close by as the gardener digs his plot, waiting for an earthworm to be disinterred, whereupon it hops down, daintily picks it up, swallows it, returning to its perch awaiting the next morsel. I have a Robin that watches me at first light when I examine my nightly catch of moths before releasing them in the undergrowth. It was some time before I realised that this feathered thief was spotting where the moths had landed and, when I turned away again to concentrate on my catch, hopped down and proceeded to reduce the population of lepidoptera in the garden. I had to develop subtle subterfuges to mislead this attentive bird. As tits have learnt how to obtain cream from the tops of milk bottles, so in the future Robins may come to take advantage of the catches of moths released from the traps of the increasing numbers of moth enthusiasts.

May

The garden has exploded into a crescendo of avian activity. I have been watching the construction of yet another Blackbirds' nest, the seventh in the garden. Two broods have fledged and one clutch was robbed, while currently there are two nests with eggs and two more under construction. I estimate that there are at least four pairs occupying a third of an acre plot. This density of worm-eaters can only be sustained by the proximity of an adjacent field of close-cut grass, which offers a limitless supply of these nutritious invertebrates. Some of the nests are only a few metres apart and frequent scraps occur as foraging birds cross each other's territories on their way to the feeding field.

I have previously stated that a pair of Long-tailed Tits was collecting what I thought was small pieces of lichen from the window-surrounds for use in the construction of their nest. On closer observation it was apparent that the material was in fact spider webs, which they use in the building of their delicate pear-shaped nests. One of the pair, probably the male, also repeatedly pecked at the glass, possibly thinking that its reflection was a rival male invading its territory.

Today a tiny bird with jerking wings and frenetic movements was displaying outside my kitchen window. It was a Goldcrest, our smallest bird. It kept flying at the window. At first I assumed it was a territorial male attacking its reflection, until its mate appeared, its golden crown tinged with orange, obviously the male. The female carried on behaving in an aggressive manner for some hours. It is fairly definite that they have a nest nearby but it is easier to find a needle in a haystack than to find the tiny delicate hammock of a Goldcrest nest high up in the cupressus.

June
I could be forgiven, if blind to the luxurious green foliage outside, for thinking it was mid-November, instead of only three weeks to mid-summer day. Today it is cold, dull and damp, in contrast to the hot sunny weather we have had recently. This grim reminder of the capricious nature

Goldcrest

of British weather has been no deterrent to the steady stream of garden birds carrying worms and caterpillars to their hungry nestlings. Some, such as Blackbirds and thrushes, have second broods close to fledging, though the latest of our summer visitors to arrive, the Spotted Flycatcher, has only just started to build its neat cup of a nest amongst the ivy on the house wall. This dapper sprite of a bird feeds on large flying insects that only become available from late spring, hence its late arrival. Unfortunately the current autumnal-like weather has grounded its quarry and the flycatcher makes dashes from its lookout perch to snatch insects, not from midair, but from the sodden foliage.

A few days ago when we were feeding the ornamental fish, my young grandson shouted that he could see a Hedgehog. I was surprised as it was in the middle of a sunny afternoon, an unusual time to see such a nocturnal animal. However he pointed to my recently renovated pond, in the middle of which was a slowly moving prickly shape. I netted the unfortunate urchin and placed it in the conservatory where, in the hothouse atmosphere, it slowly recovered from hypothermia. After several hours, at dusk, I placed it outside on the lawn and was pleased to see it slowly uncurl and quietly sidle away into the bushes. Although Hedgehogs are good swimmers it would have found it impossible to get a grip on the smooth slippery pond-liner to drag itself out. The moral of this story is that we should check our ponds at least daily for any unfortunate victims, or better still provide some kind of escape route to enable any trapped mammal or bird to extricate itself from a watery death. Initially I thought the poor creature must have spent at least twelve hours in the water after falling in. However on several occasions during the last few days, a Hedgehog has been seen foraging in the garden in broad daylight, so in fact it could have fallen into the water only a short time before, during a daytime ramble.

July
No wonder we British are always talking about the weather. This spring and summer we have been subjected to long, cool, wet and windy periods, alternating with short bursts of hot and humid weather. In spite of these changeable conditions the garden birds have enjoyed a successful nesting season. In fact an hour ago I discovered a Robins' nest only a metre from

my front door. It contained three nestlings nearly ready to fledge. I find it incredible that these confiding birds had built a nest, laid eggs, incubated them for nearly two weeks and reared them near to fledging before I discovered them, in spite of my twice-daily walk round the garden looking for any such developments.

The weather has had a greater effect on the local butterflies. I have seen very few this spring, either in the garden or in the neighbouring countryside. However the short hot spell a week or so ago produced a scattering of migrants, notably Red Admirals and Painted Ladies, only a singleton of each visiting my garden. I have a forlorn hope that a particular migrant, the self-descriptive Clouded Yellow butterfly, may grace my garden, as I recently saw two individuals in a nearby wood. This beautiful insect is the butterfly equivalent of the avian Waxwing in that it appears in considerable numbers in particular years, often after a number of years with not a single sighting. To see two individuals in inland Cumbria in June is unusual, and other observers have made further sightings. Keep a lookout for a Cabbage White-sized butterfly, which always perches with closed wings, so only the deep yellow underwings are seen. There is a dark spot on the forewing and silver spots on the hindwing. Other migrant insects have visited the garden, including the day-flying Silver-Y Moth, buzzing, brown and heavy-bodied.

Amongst the many birds that visit the bird-table is a Jackdaw. It has developed the trick of lifting the tit-feeder off its nail, and when it falls to the ground it levers off the top and snaffles the nuts. As I am a spoilsport I made the feeder more secure.

A mass exodus is now taking place from the ponds. Dozens of tiny froglets and toadlets are leaving the water and moving into the long grass. Here they will find their prey, including minute spiders.

August
One of the first things I do when arriving home from a holiday is to make a check on the garden to see how all its inhabitants, both animals and plants, are faring. I check to see if eggs have been laid or have hatched and whether young birds have fledged, and to note any changes have taken place. When I walked around the large pond I did not see a single fish. Initially I assumed my absence of a fortnight had caused the fish to

change their habit of swimming up to be fed. However after several days without sighting a single one, I began to fear the worst. I did not believe they had been stolen, as there was no sign of disturbance either around or in the pond. My suspicions were confirmed when a neighbours told me that they had seen a Heron in the area when we were away. They said that their ornamental fish, valuable carp protected by netting, had gone into hiding as a result, they thought, of being scared by the Heron. I was completely resigned to the loss of my ornamental fish until a few days later, when, after a warm afternoon, they all appeared and started feeding vigorously. It is not clear to me whether they hid during this protracted period as a result of being frightened by a Heron or whether they had gone into a torpid state as a result of the recent unseasonable cool spell, or both. Even the father of the prodigal son could not have been more overjoyed than I was at the reappearance of my lost fish. I am pleased to have any wildlife visitors to my garden, though sometimes the activities of Herons, Sparrowhawks and Moles make them less than welcome.

Blackbirds and thrushes are finding it increasingly difficult to reach their worm prey, coiled up deep in the desiccated soil. Now is the time when these carnivorous birds augment their diet with soft fruits such as blackcurrants and raspberries. I do not cover my bushes and canes with netting. As well as denying these songbirds much needed sustenance, the nets can become death traps if the birds get their feet tangled in the fine mesh.

September

The last few nights there has been a chill in the air and a lingering mist in the morning. Autumn is around the corner, though Painted Ladies, Red Admirals, Small Tortoiseshells and Peacocks are still nectaring on the buddleia. The Robin is singing its plaintive winter song and marauding flocks of garrulous Starlings descend to devour the ripening elderberries in the hedge.

The dry weather brought the Hedgehog out well before dark, scavenging for the reduced supply of slugs, but recent rains have encouraged the emergence of these destructive gastropods and the Hedgehog is no longer seen in the daytime. It can catch sufficient numbers of its slimy prey during the hours of darkness.

A length of hedge along a nearby roadside has been slashed back, destroying its ripening crop of hips, haws and other berries. They would have provided food for our local finches. The hedgerows are the food-reservoirs for much of our wildlife. However a housing development is taking place in our community and the resulting gardens with their shrubs, hedges and bird-tables may redress the balance and encourage an increase in birds, insects and small mammals.

October

The advent of more changeable autumnal weather has brought to an end the late summer plague of wasps. A few weeks ago I had to pluck up courage to harvest plums and early ripening apples in the fruit garden. Some of the Victoria plums, still hanging on their twigs, were almost completely eaten away by a festering scrum of wasps. What appeared to be innocent rosy apple windfalls were packed with seething wads of these angry insects. I was lucky to get away with only two stings. The discomforts of the central African bush are as nothing compared to an English wild garden with its attendant wasps, brambles and nettles! But we do not have to be concerned about leopards lurking in the laburnum.

I have had several reports of both Comma and Clouded Yellow butterflies in and around local gardens. The Clouded Yellow is purely a migrant in our area, though it has recently bred on the south coast. However, it appears that the Comma is establishing itself here. I heard a report that four were seen together on the same buddleia bush. Hopefully this increase of sightings is not solely the result of a seasonal influx of migrants but also due to successful breeding locally.

It is again the season of the fungal foray when parties of enthusiasts creep head-down through the woods peeling and sniffing at specimens of this incredibly diverse group of organisms. My garden is host to various species, to most of which I cannot give a name, but I have been lucky to have a mushroom colony situated under some cupressus. Each year a few of their aniseed-scented fruiting bodies have risen phoenix-like from the leaf debris. This year there have been several eruptions. As I harvested one crop another started to develop. I have timed their period of growth, about nine days, from 'knob' to flat 'umbrella'. I also found that copious watering of the developing fungi did not accelerate their maturation. I used to think that mushrooms 'mushroomed' overnight and pickers would set out at dawn to reap this ephemeral crop, which was not available the previous night. We should always question old tales and make our own observations to determine the truth.

Some weeks ago I cleaned out one of my small ponds. In it were lurking three Shubunkins that I had not seen for a year. My motivation was primarily to make it a wild pond, but also to satisfy my curiosity as to the fate of these fancy fish. I found the three fat healthy specimens much increased in size. I placed them in the pond that contained a mixed collection of lively Goldfish and Golden Orfe, survivors of a Heron attack. The temperament of the Shubunkins, previously lethargic and secretive, completely changed. They started actively swimming in full view and coming to the surface to be fed and even began chasing the original inhabitants of the pond. Fish, like people, can sometimes benefit from both a move, and a change in company!

November
What a summer it has been for the growth of vegetation. The trees and bushes on the south side of the garden have grown several feet during the damp summer and have once again plunged a large area, including the ponds, into shade. I have trimmed and pruned but drastic action was required with lopping of all the birch and cupressus trees to head height. This required the use of a chain-saw in the hands of a professional. Fortunately the operation was carried out during two consecutive dry days, a rarity during the current monsoon conditions. If trees are pollarded at this height they can be easily managed by annual pruning with long-handled secateurs, even by an increasingly enfeebled gardener. The shock of being able to see beyond the confines of the garden and the loss of a certain amount of privacy is compensated by the knowledge that next spring the extra light will be beneficial for the garden plants. In particular the ponds will be healthier as the oxygenating plants will photosynthesise more efficiently, so improving the oxygen content of the water to the benefit of aquatic life. Light-loving water-lilies should produce more blooms. Soon I will be anchoring netting over the ponds in order to stop the leaves polluting the water. As water always finds the lowest level, so leaves always find a pond. Once in, they never blow out!

All the migrants have left for southern climes, but the recent mild weather has deceived some resident birds into thinking that it is spring. A few days ago a Song Thrush burst into song, and up to a week ago many Red Admiral Butterflies were sunning themselves in the autumn sunshine.

December
The trunks of the recently pollarded trees were cut into logs and stacked into piles and so will provide food and shelter for a multitude of minibeasts. The branches were banked up against the hedge, again to form a wildlife haven for small mammals such as Hedgehogs, shrews and mice. Branches and logs should not be burnt, for as well as causing pollution and annoyance to neighbours, many small garden denizens are denied food and cover. I used some of the logs as edging around one of my ponds.

Continuous rain has turned the garden into a quagmire but the absence of frost has allowed my little mushroom patch to carry on producing more fruiting bodies, albeit of a smaller size. I must have picked and enjoyed several pounds, yet I have hardly seen a single one in the surrounding fields. It will be interesting to see if this manna from heaven phenomenon is repeated next year.

The Fieldfares have arrived and are chattering away as they strip the hips and haws from the high hedge and a stately cock Pheasant regularly stalks the lawn. It pecks at large grains of wheat which have been scattered under the bird-table. Commercially sold wild bird food consists of many different types of seed, including millet, wheat and rolled maize, each one suitable for a particular bird species. I find this mixture to be invaluable for feeding the garden birds and the use of it is non-controversial. Strict hygiene is essential. Any peanuts that have not been eaten after a few days should be discarded and the feeders cleaned and sterilised.

2001

Common Frog

January

After a mild, wet and windy autumn, it comes as a shock to the system when frost and snow arrive, but at least we have warm accommodation as well as food and drink. Not so for our non-migratory garden birds, and neither can they hibernate like some mammals. Until now these birds have found sufficient food in the soft ground of field and lawn, but are now denied access to worms and other invertebrates by the concrete-hard ground. Now is the time to provide insect-eating birds like tits and Dunnocks with a regular source of food at bird-tables. However there are still sufficient berries in the hedgerows for our resident Blackbirds and Thrushes as well as Redwings and Fieldfares, visitors from northern Europe. A small flock of the latter birds has been feeding on left over apples. Don't be too tidy, leave any unwanted windfalls for the birds.

A few days ago, just before the water in the birdbath turned into a block of ice, I watched a Robin bathing. It was at dusk and near freezing. The sight of this little bird, with its wire-thin legs, splashing the water under its feathers, made me shudder. It seemed oblivious to the cold. Being clean and keeping its feathers in operational order, is of paramount importance to a bird.

February

A few days ago I managed with considerable effort and not a little danger to life and limb to place a long wooden box-like structure fairly high up in the beech tree at the bottom of the garden. It was an owl nest box, known as a 'chimney box'. The structure measured 80 cm long and was 25 cm square. It was attached to a sloping branch at an angle of about 30 degrees to the vertical with its open top inclined to the northeast, facing away from the prevailing southwesterly winds. I am not very hopeful that an owl will choose to nest in it, even though they are heard around the house. At least provision has been made for that possibility, or other large hole-nesting birds such as Stock Doves or Jackdaws could choose to nest there.

Already I have observed Blue Tits inspecting the nest-boxes in the garden. I will make certain that all debris, along with accompanying 'creepies', have been removed from boxes that were occupied last year. New boxes can be constructed and placed in the garden, preferably well before St Valentine's Day.

During the recent period of protracted frost I had omitted to break the ice in a pond which did not contain fish. At the end of the thaw I found several dead frogs floating on the surface. I emptied the pond, suspecting a leak in the liner as the water level had fallen during the thaw. I was dismayed to find upwards of another fifty dead frogs. In future I will make certain that all the ponds are allowed to 'breathe' during icy weather, so saving the lives of frogs hibernating in the mud at the bottom.

A neighbour reported to me that three Waxwings had been in his garden for several days. These pretty birds are often found at this time of year in the vicinity of supermarkets, the attraction being not bargains but the berried shrubs planted on the landscaped sites. On a recent walk around the village, I noticed that hardly a berry remained on the hedgerows, and the fields seemed lifeless. Now is the time of year when many birds leave the countryside for town and village gardens in quest of food on bird-tables and in feeders. I hope that when they visit your garden they will not be disappointed.

March

The flowering snowdrops and crocuses have been given a sharp reminder lately that winter has not ended. Frosty and snowy weather does not seem to affect the snowdrops, but the crocuses have a decided wilting look about them. The cold snap has also caused a mass invasion of tits and finches to the garden. They are quickly lowering the level of peanuts in the tit-feeder and clearing the bird-table of the wild bird food. This consists of a mixture of seeds and each bird species has its preference. The small birds devour all the tiny seeds but none appear to manage the large husked ears of wheat, though sometimes the Collared Doves make an attempt. A cock Pheasant visits the garden but because of its lack of agility or perhaps its reluctance to forfeit some of its dignity, it never attempts to fly onto the bird-table. I flicked the wheat seeds onto the ground for its convenience and it showed its appreciation by haughtily stalking underneath the table and pecking up the offerings. I was pleased to see the resident pair of Woodpigeons accompanying it, quickly hoovering up all the remaining seeds. Incidentally, what beautiful birds Woodpigeons are when viewed close to, with their dove-grey plumage and ornate neck-ring, which gives them their alternative name of 'Ring Dove'.

Among the species of bird that have become visitors to the tit-feeder only over the last few years is the Long-tailed Tit. Several have visited the feeder over the last few days and yesterday five hung all together on the one feeder, an exciting spectacle.

There were signs of spring some days ago. On 21st February frogs were moving in the ponds. On the same day a neighbour reported that there was frogspawn in his pond. Unfortunately I have found that ice can kill off the spawn and the chances of survival of any spawn laid before this last cold spell are low. The capricious nature of our climate means that there is no clear change from winter to spring and there are many false starts. This is often to the detriment of hibernating creatures. Small Tortoiseshell butterflies in particular can awake during a mild spell, use up all their energy reserves, and die when winter resumes.

In spite of the cold, bird activity increases as the days lengthen. On 23rd February I watched a House Sparrow collecting dry grasses, then flying to the ivy on the side of the house where it is beginning to build its untidy woven nest. Repetitive strident calls of the Song Thrush have been heard for the last month, whatever the weather. The mellow fluting call of the Blackbird, evocative of the milder evenings of spring, has yet to be heard.

April

I have been watching a Magpie moving about in the high hawthorn hedge outside the window. Whether it is searching for early songbird nests or reconnoitring for a nest-site I do not know. As it is on its own it signifies sorrow, according to the old rhyme. This state of mind not only reflects one's own frustration at being denied access to footpaths and woodland areas due to the current foot-and-mouth crisis, but also the complete lack of a journey into spring during the month of March. Except for the flowering of the spring bulbs, and the odd pale yellow star of a lesser celandine there has been little evidence of any greening of shrubs or hedgerows.

For nearly six weeks frogs have been evident in the ponds and yet to date there has been no sign of spawn. There have been persistent overnight frosts, which must have delayed their spawning. I have also noticed that most of the frogs are male. I have only seen two couples. I previously mentioned that after Christmas sixty frogs died in one of the ponds at the end of a hard and protracted frost. Many of these were females. I wonder if a disproportionate number of females died, perhaps due to gender differences in methods of hibernation.

In spite of the inhospitable weather, nesting activity has begun. I watched both a Song Thrush and a Blackbird collecting soggy grasses from around the pond. I had been a bit too 'garden proud' in clearing away loose dead vegetation and the birds were having trouble wrenching the less yielding material from the ground. Don't be too tidy! Leave some loose material about for the birds to build their nests. The Song Thrush

Lesser Celandine

flew into a nearby holly bush, but to my dismay the Blackbird flew off with building material into a neighbour's garden. I get quite possessive about 'my' birds.

Several times recently I have been startled by a loud thud caused by a male Blackbird crashing into the window, the result of two sparring males chasing each other whilst establishing their territories. Each morning as I draw the curtains I notice two Robins fly away. They have built their nest in a crude homemade open-fronted nest-box against the window. The box is quite large, but the tenants have built their mossy cup of a nest in one half, filling the rest of the box with dead leaves.

The habits of the different visitors to the bird-table continue to hold my attention. Of particular note are the actions of the Coal Tits. They dash in, grab a morsel and dash off again, unlike the sustained feeding of their Great and Blue cousins. The increasing frequency of visits of Goldfinches and Long-tailed Tits to the nut-feeders is worth recording. I also note in late winter the first arrivals of Siskins to the nut-feeders. I have only had males visiting this year.

On entering the garden one morning recently a strong rank smell

114

assailed my nostrils. It was only the second time I had had a visit from a Fox. Such garden visits appear to be quite rare in our area. When staying with friends in other parts of the country I have found that such visits are quite commonplace.

Hopefully it will not be too long before the terrible affliction of foot-and-mouth is over and we can get back into the forests and onto the fells again. Until then we will have to spend more time in our gardens and take the opportunity to make them even more friendly for wildlife.

May

About this time each year I always seem to say that this is the worst spring I can remember, but this year I am sure that it is! The trees are still mostly devoid of any greenery and how the recently arrived Swallows are surviving the sleety rain and absence of any flying insects I cannot imagine. The weather has apparently not dampened the spirits of the worm-eating birds such as Blackbirds and Robins. Two pairs of the latter are feeding young in artificial nest-sites. One nest is in a crudely made box. It contains three rapidly expanding pot-bellied chicks. On the top of this box is a Blackbird's nest containing four equally pot-bellied nestlings. The relative position of these two nests reminds me of a sea anemone on top of a whelk shell containing a hermit crab, though in the scenario in the garden there appears to be no mutual benefit. In fact the actions of four foraging parent birds is more likely to attract the unwelcome attention of cats. Several other birds are nesting, including a Starling sitting on seven beautiful eggs in a box that I made from a drawer. A Great Tit is incubating its clutch of seven eggs. Tits tend to time the hatching of their chicks to coincide with the availability of an abundance of caterpillars, which feed on freshly unfurled leaves. They had better hurry up and unfurl or there will be many very hungry young tits.

Another indicator of the slowness of the season is that frogspawn was laid extremely late. Because of the coldness of the water it has taken an extremely long time to develop. Only recently have the tadpoles left their jelly. Because of the extremely protracted spawning period, the plants and mud in one of the small ponds were stirred up to such an extent that I decided to clean it out. I carefully placed the spawn and indignant amphibians in buckets. From this tiny pond, specimens of five species of amphibian were rescued! Common Frogs, Toads and Palmate, Smooth and Great Crested Newts were placed back into the pond.

It is interesting to see what wildlife can be found in a garden pond. A dark night and a powerful torch are the ingredients of a successful newt survey. It is under cover of darkness that these shy hunters leave the safety of the weeds to forage in the open water, when the hungry Herons are asleep in their treetop homes.

June

The protracted period that the spawning frogs spent in the company of the ornamental fish was detrimental to the latter. Behind the fishes' gills were areas devoid of scales, and this puzzled me. The reason for this became clear when I discovered that an amorous amphibian had clasped an unfortunate fish in a vice like grip, in the erroneous assumption that it was a female frog.

Unwelcome early morning visits from a Heron continue. I thought that because I had not seen the goldfish for some days they had been 'spooked'. It is clear now that, rather than hiding at the bottom of the pond, they are in fact in the Heron's stomach. I was amazed that it had taken the fish, in spite of the pond being full of thick weed and the water being up to two feet deep. My antipathy towards this lanky bandit has been increased by the fact that it still visits my fishless pond in order to remove frogs and newts. In the process it disturbs the water plants, and has twice overturned the basket containing a repotted water lily. It is a test of my love of wildlife that murderous thoughts of revenge are repressed.

I was sad to find a prickly mound on the lawn. A large Hedgehog looked well fed, yet it was dead. Its demise could have been caused by the use of slug pellets. The unfortunate insectivore had perhaps eaten slugs killed by pellets. A Hedgehog can be a more successful controller of these ravenous molluscs than any chemical. It may be that the reduction of Song Thrush numbers in some areas could be in part due to use of this insecticide. If slug pellets must be used it would be better to cover them in such a way as to make them accessible to slugs but not to birds or Hedgehogs.

On 10th June I was excited to find a brood of small caterpillars in a web on a clump of nettles. Initially I thought they were Small Tortoiseshell larvae until they shed their skins, when they became much darker and were undoubtedly Peacock caterpillars. It is of course nice to have Peacocks breeding in the garden, but I was slightly disappointed. Small Tortoiseshell butterflies have become quite scarce during the last year or two. The nettle patch chosen was in full sun, a situation in which the gravid female always prefers to lay her eggs. The caterpillars of these attractive butterflies will never be found on nettles growing in shady places, though several species of moth are not so choosy.

A couple of weeks ago an unusual bird, the size and shape of a small crow, arrived in the garden. It had white secondary feathers on its wings and a partly white tail, some of the feathers of which were longer on one side than the other. It looked like a cross between a magpie and a carrion crow. This 'Cragpie', as I named it, was extremely tame. When mobbed by a passing Rook, it flew towards me as if for protection. Its crow family relations all appear to hate it. It has been hanging around the garden, using it as its base. I wonder whether it has been hand reared.

July

A month later and the Cragpie is still alive and fluttering. It strides about the lawn and can manage just enough aerial ability to flop over the hedge into a neighbour's garden. It is still tormented by its fellow corvids and on the approach of a Rook from the village rookery either makes a clumsy attempt to find cover or flies in my direction as if for safety.

The mystery about its origin has deepened. A lady who lives in Upperby said she had an identical Cragpie in her garden, which she had rescued from a nearby nest. Its behaviour was identical to the one in the garden. The mystery was later compounded when she rang to say that yet another Cragpie was to be seen around her son's place of business on London Road. It seemed incredible that there are three of these curious corvids. It would be interesting to know of the existence of any others.

One evening I caught a glimpse of a large grey shape lifting over the ponds. The Heron did not land as it obviously had intended to do but changed its mind and with wide straining wings laboriously gained height to clear the surrounding trees. Its change of plan was due to a plastic heron standing realistically at the margin of the large pond. I have previously mentioned how a visiting Heron had taken all the ornamental fish. This was shortly after I had thrown away the remains of an ornamental heron that had stood by the pond for years. For the fish to be taken so soon after I had removed the original plastic effigy seemed proof enough of the deterrent effect of such an ornament. Herons are not sociable animals and are dissuaded from entering a territory already occupied by another fishing bird. This may seem like locking the proverbial stable door, but hopefully it will protect the amphibians from unwelcome attention.

During the spring a pair of Goldfinches has graced the garden. These dainty eaters of dandelion seeds with their liquid calls and their gold-and-red livery were certain to be nesting in my garden, but where? On 23rd June I was pleased to see a fledgling Goldfinch being fed by its parent on the telephone wire above the garden, confirming successful breeding.

We have passed the summer solstice and as if on queue many of our songbirds have ceased singing. The dense vegetation is full of young birds and in the evening the flowering honeysuckle is attended by its crepuscular visitors, the moths.

August

The last few days have been hot and sunny in contrast to the cool, damp weather of only a week ago. Very quickly the ground is drying out and the earthworms have burrowed deep. It is fortunate for the Blackbirds and Song Thrushes that the season of blackcurrants and raspberries is here, and these soft fruits will sustain them over the period when their staple diet of worms is denied to them. A greatly increased population of tits and finches, a result of a successful breeding season, are rapidly emptying the tit-feeders on the bird-table. Don't stop feeding your garden birds in the summer! The lack of food available in the surrounding farmland, and their increased numbers at this season, make it imperative to continue feeding all the year round.

The bird-table receives two visitors of a non-avian kind. Each evening an hour before sundown a shuffling ball of spines trundles out from the adjacent hedge to hoover up any scraps that have fallen on the ground. The Hedgehog has come for its supper. I place a plate of leftovers near it. After initially rolling up, it soon uncurls and tucks in. If I had placed the scraps out earlier, in anticipation of its later arrival, the neighbourhood cats would have quickly devoured them. The other visitor is a Bank Vole. This little brown rodent is not unlike a miniature guinea pig, with a blunt snout and a relatively short tail. It has become quite tame and I can watch it only a few feet away as it holds seeds fallen from the table above in its forepaws, nibbling neatly.

September

The garden is completely silent. No birds are singing, as there is now no need to attract a mate or defend a nesting territory. The froglets and toadlets have left the ponds and I have to be careful not to inflict unwitting amputations on unfortunate amphibians when strimming the long grass on the lawn edge. In recent days however I have been pleased at the number of butterflies that are visiting flowers in the garden. All three species of white butterfly are present. Most of them are Large Whites, which outnumber the usually more common Green-veined Whites and Small Whites. The last two are of similar size but the Green-veined White, as its name suggests, has green 'veins' on the underside of its hindwings. The caterpillars of the Small and Large Whites prefer cabbages and other brassicas, while the larvae of the Green-veined White prefer the leaves of various wild cresses. Other butterflies at present in the garden include Small Tortoiseshells and Peacocks. The caterpillars of both these brightly coloured butterflies feed on nettles. Ideally a wild life garden should have a nettle patch in a sunny position for these butterflies, for Red Admirals and, if lucky, Commas. I have yet to see any in my garden.

As well as the absence of bird song, other indicators signify the approaching end of summer and the beginning of autumn. The first mushrooms are appearing and species of moth indicative of the back end of the year are turning up in the moth-traps. The Cragpie still visits, but it spends most of its time in the garden of a neighbour, who feeds it regularly. It appears to be losing some of its white feathers and becoming more crow-like, but only in appearance, not behaviour. It is still reluctant to fly and remains very confiding. It will be interesting to see how long it will survive before it becomes cat fodder.

October

The summer has come to an end. Most of our summer visitors have left and with the exception of such birds as the Collared Doves, the nesting season has finished. Heavy dews greet us each morning, making it much later before the sun, if there is any, burns off the moisture and the lawn can be mown. As yet the winter visitors such as Redwings and Fieldfares have not arrived.

Now is the time to take stock and review plans for making our gardens more attractive for wildlife in the coming year. The garden can be made more hospitable to birds by providing food during the winter, cover for nesting sites and water for drinking and cleaning feathers. Plants that provide berries or hips for birds include cotoneaster, elder, guelder rose, honeysuckle, pyracanthus and rowan. Flowers which should be allowed to go to seed include crane's-bill, clematis, globe thistle, honesty and sunflower.

Butterflies can be attracted to the garden by growing flowers rich in nectar. These include butterfly bush (buddleia), candytuft, goldenrod, marjoram, iceplant, Michaelmas daisy, and sweet rocket. They flower at different times of the year, so supplying a ready source of nectar from spring to autumn. Moths, night-flying cousins of butterflies, can be attracted to the garden by the provision of night-scented flowers such as honeysuckle, red valerian, jasmine, night-scented stock and evening primrose.

November
It is 1st November and only in the last couple of days have we had anything that resembles autumnal weather. There has been no frost. Gaudy begonias and other tender border plants are still in full bloom. In this topsy-turvy climate some wild flowers don't seem to know what season it is. A few days ago down at Leighton Moss on the edge of Morecambe Bay I saw a clump of marsh marigolds in full bloom. Their normal flowering period is spring and early summer. Recently there has been a huge influx of Red Admiral butterflies. Particularly attractive for them are the nectar-laden flowers of ivy, which also attract another migrant, the Silver-Y moth. In spite of the recent extremely mild weather, our summer visitors, such as Swallows and Martins, have left. Perhaps the shortening length of day is more important than temperature in triggering their departure.

One morning recently it was much cooler and with the fresher wind I heard the chatter of our first winter visitors, Fieldfares. They settled on the hawthorn hedge and started to demolish the berries. The recent strong winds have been blowing apples from the trees. Don't be too tidy and clean them all up! When cold weather eventually arrives they will provide nourishment for Blackbirds and thrushes and for the winter visitors. In previous years windfalls were quickly consumed by crawling clumps of wasps. This year there have been no wasps' nests in the garden and I have seen very few of these troublesome insects.

Birds, like humans, prefer nuts that are fresh. If you keep topping up the feeder, nuts can remain in the bottom and become mouldy, particularly during the recent damp mild weather. When I need to top up the feeders, I tip out the remaining nuts and partly fill the feeder with fresh nuts and then place the older nuts on top so that they will be consumed first. After some time it is best to give the feeder a good wash. We would not like to eat a meal off plates that had not been washed for months. We would soon become ill, and so can the birds.

As in other autumns the fairy ring of mushrooms has reappeared. It gets bigger each year and produces several pounds of this delicious fungus to fry with my bacon. It remains a mystery to me why this patch appears in this one place without fail each autumn. I have not been able to move part of its mycelium successfully to other parts of the garden.

The Cragpie has gone. I have seen neither hide nor feather of this curious creature for the last week. It has left the village, having eventually lost its remaining white feathers. It could be that it has finally been accepted by the neighbourhood crows and Rooks as one of them. Birds, like people, are often suspicious of any variation from the norm.

December
Except for a couple of days of snowy weather in the second week of November, the weather has been unusually mild. Honeysuckle has been flowering and two viburnum bushes have been in bloom. One variety flowers in December, but the adjacent bush usually flowers in April! Grass has continued growing and azaleas are in bloom. We live in a temperate country where we expect four seasons in the year, but not every month! The pond plants have also continued to grow. Because of the dense aquatic vegetation I have not needed to cover the ponds with netting to catch the wind-blown leaves. They cannot sink as they are trapped on

the surface of the ponds and are easily removed by hand. The invasive antipodean waterweed, *Crassula helmsii*, or pigmyweed, is spreading like wildfire in the large pond and needs to be removed.

There were two 'firsts' in the garden in late November. I watched what I at first thought was a female Chaffinch on the bird-table. It was slightly more colourful however, with a white rump and dark stripes on its crown, a female Brambling. I had been looking out for this winter visitor in its usual haunts. At Talkin Tarn in some winters flocks can be seen in the beech trees eating beech mast. Ironically the first one I have seen this autumn is on my own bird-table. These usually gregarious finches breed in Scandinavia but often winter in Britain. They can sometimes be seen in mixed flocks with Chaffinches.

The other 'first' was a Nuthatch. This stubby active tree-climbing bird with its powerful pointed bill cannot be confused with any other. My visitor flew back and forth collecting sunflower seeds, which I assume it would be cracking open under cover in an adjacent bush. This individual continued to visit the bird-table for about a week. I hope it will remain until spring and, with a mate, nest in one of my boxes. I remember these attractive little birds fifty years ago on the edge of the North York moors at a latitude not much different from that of north Cumbria, yet it is only recently that they have moved into our area.

2002

Foxglove

January

A welcome visitor to the bird table is the Great Spotted Woodpecker, with its undulating flight and sharp *'tchich'* call. For many years I had not seen one in the garden but this thrush-sized black and white bird now visits quite frequently. The more frequent sightings may reflect an increase in the local population of this interesting bird, perhaps because of the recent practice of allowing mature trees to die and slowly decay. Decaying trees provide invertebrates as food and soft wood for nest-holes.

Some weeks ago I obtained two damaged and abandoned owl nest-boxes. I have repaired them and placed them in strategic places in the garden. I had already placed a home-made box in a large beech tree. The fact of having three boxes does not mean I expect to have three pairs of owls nesting. Owls are anything but colonial nesters. It is to give them more choice. Each box is placed in a different situation, two being in exposed positions, while the third is hidden in a dense cupressus. The literature gives the ideal internal dimensions of a 'chimney-style' box as 78 cm x 23 cm x 23 cm, open at the upper end. My two new boxes are somewhat smaller, so I wonder whether an owl will take to one. I have seen an owl nest in a hollow birch whose girth hardly seemed any greater than that of its occupant. On most nights in December I heard owls calling, often within the garden itself, and sometimes in the same bush in which one of the nest-boxes is situated. Two different calls, *'kee-wick'* and *'hoo-oo-oo-oo'*, were made, signifying the probability of both the male and female being present. Both can make either call, but an individual never makes the two calls together.

An interest one can develop in the wildlife garden is the observation of firsts and lasts in nature, or phenology. There is a scientifically based study run by the Woodland Trust but we can make a start by noting when the first flower of a common species opens or the date when the first migrant bird arrives in our gardens in the spring. The idea is to record the dates over a period of years and note any long-term variations. Such variations could well be indicators of climate change.

February

At 9 a.m. on 29th January a Song Thrush was in full song in the garden, one of the first indicators of the coming spring. The weather has been extremely mild for the last few weeks, albeit very stormy, and one wonders what effect this will have on the garden wildlife. I have heard reports of Peacock and Small Tortoiseshell butterflies coming out of hibernation and fluttering against windows. They are wastefully burning up their stored energy, which should have sustained them over the winter. I wonder if it would be better to place them in a container in the fridge during spells of extremely mild weather.

Long-tailed Field-mice have been raiding the sack of peanuts stored in the cellar. Most nuts were not devoured *in situ* but taken to a far corner to be eaten, the evidence being the discarded husks. I was surprised that they had transported the nuts, as a hamster might, because they lack the cheek pouches of the latter. The peanuts were chosen in preference to mixed bird food and sunflower seeds stored nearby. Needless to say I have now placed all the food in lidded plastic tubs to thwart any future felony.

A few weeks ago I observed that the nuts in the tit-feeders were not diminishing. Thinking that the wind and rain had caused them to swell and to become unpalatable or difficult to access, I decided upon a simple experiment. I tipped all the uneaten nuts into one feeder and filled the other feeder with fresh dry nuts. In neither feeder did the levels go down. Obviously the exposure of the nuts to the weather was not the reason for their unpopularity with the tits. After some days the birds returned to the feeders and the nuts in both feeders were equally popular. It is interesting to carry out experiments in the wildlife garden, however simple.

March

For the last few days I have not set foot on my lawn for fear of sinking into the mud. I have never known so much rain in this country. As spring approaches it remains to be seen whether the heavy rain has affected the garden wildlife.

A predated Collared Dove's egg, with a small hole in its shell, lay below its nest in the high cupressus hedge. All the contents had been removed. The hole was too small to be made by a Carrion Crow or perhaps even a Magpie, another garden mystery. A second pair of these small pigeons has built a nest on top of an old Woodpigeons' nest, right up against an owl box. Two glossy and almost round eggs lay in the nest.

Several weeks ago there was a slight movement and a show of bubbles in one of the ponds, the first stirring of hibernating frogs. By the evening, after a very mild day with strong winds, the whole pond was a seething mass of amphibian frivolity. The following day, however, when the wind changed to the northwest, the frogs disappeared and I have not seen them since. The colony of frogs in a garden pond half a mile away at the same altitude and in a similar situation, always manages to produce spawn up to a month before my frogs do. It could be that there is some genetic difference between the two colonies. My colony originally came as tadpoles from Penrith, which lies at a higher altitude. It might be interesting to swap a few individuals between the two ponds and monitor the results.

125

Recently the tit-feeders have been visited by a party of Long-tailed Tits, as well as by Goldfinches. Only the occasional Siskin has visited the nuts this year. If one is not able to identify common garden birds by their appearance, observing the way they feed is a great help. I have seen many Rooks visit the bird-table from the nearby rookery, but never Carrion Crows. These birds are very wary and although they visit the garden, they keep their distance. A tiny tit, which always flies away from the bird-table to consume its nut elsewhere, is likely to be a Coal Tit. A small finch that always hangs upside down on the tit-feeder could be a Siskin. The sparrow-sized bird hopping quietly about under the bird-table picking up tiny morsels in its fine beak is a Dunnock, or Hedge Accentor. Incidentally, the Dunnock is often called a Hedge-sparrow. Modern pedants, who forget that 'sparrow' was often used as a generic name for small birds, frown upon the latter name. Likewise the term 'wren' was used for all very small birds. It is also the case that a term of endearment can become the common name for a bird – thus Redbreast, then Robin Redbreast, and finally just Robin. In years to come we might refer to a Wren as a 'Jenny'. A Robin (redbreast) by any other name sings just as sweet.

April
My colony of frogs must be unique. They are the last to spawn in the area. The first clump of spawn appeared on 20th March, a month later than that produced by colonies in neighbouring ponds. As well as the purring croak of the frogs I can hear the piping of a Common Toad. These warty amphibians usually spawn a week or so later than the frogs. Presumably they require a higher spawning temperature than do their cousins.

Outside the study window I have been watching a Wren building its domed nest in the ivy on the house wall. He – I know it is a he as only males build the nests – is carrying large dead leaves. Male Wrens build several cock nests and the female then selects one and lines it with feathers. I hope she chooses the one outside my window so that I may observe the rearing of a large brood of nestlings. A Blackbird is building a nest three feet above the Wrens' nest. Several other birds have been collecting nesting material, including a Carrion Crow. It spends ages pulling and twisting at fine birch branches. Why this energetic bird does not collect dead material from the ground puzzles me, as it expends a considerable amount of energy in tearing off the twigs.

Some moths have been coming to my trap for the last few nights, after many mothless weeks. One is an attractive largish moth called the Oak Beauty. Many are of the 'Quaker' group of moths, so-called because of their sober appearance and cryptic coloration. Their appearance coincides with the opening of sallow and willow blossoms, including pussy willow, on which they feed. If a torch is shone into sallow bushes an hour after dark on a mild, still night the reward might be the spectacle of various species of moth feeding on the blossoms. The most strongly marked and one of the most common of these moths is the Hebrew Character. In spite of the descriptive inference of its vernacular name, its specific name, *gothica,* refers to the mark like an arch on its forewing. It in fact looks more Norman than Gothic.

Some days ago I noticed a cloud of feathers floating by the window. There was a chorus of alarm notes and frantic activity amongst all the songbirds in the area. The cause of this commotion was a Sparrowhawk. It had made a strike at a Collared Dove, which was perching nearby, ruffled but uninjured. It might have been one of the parents of the single squab in the nest against the owl box. One of the two eggs had failed to hatch and the single nestling sat smug and self-satisfied in the middle of its platform of a nest, the sole concern of its devoted parents. Its appearance before it developed feathers was that of a tiny Dodo. The long extinct Dodo was of course a giant flightless pigeon.

May

The Collared Dove nestling grew rapidly and was seen fully-grown, perching on the edge of its nest. An hour later I found it dead but still warm on the ground. Initially there appeared to be no injury, but on closer examination tiny spots of blood could be seen on its back and the skin appeared to have been punctured as if by needles. Similar traces of blood and puncture marks were found on the underside of its body. I surmised that it had been grabbed by a raptor, possibly a Sparrowhawk, which had flown off when I approached. The bird may have literally died of shock, as the wounds did not appear to be fatal.

For the last three weeks an owl has become a resident in the high cupressus hedge adjoining the house. Its presence is made obvious by the vociferous alarm notes of the nesting garden birds. This warning chorus becomes strident at dusk when the nocturnal hunter stirs itself for the night's foraging. For the first few days it roosted in full view, six feet above a Collared Dove brooding two eggs. The dove seemed unperturbed by the proximity of its sleeping companion. When the owl moved away to another roosting site the dove's eggs were taken. Perhaps the presence of the owl had given the dove some protection. The owl left a legacy of several pellets under its roost. These initiated an examination by a pair of budding young pathologists, who dissected out a charnel house of bones, fur and skulls, mostly of Long-tailed Field-mice. The behaviour of this bird is an enigma, as it often lets out a hoot in the middle of the day. On discussing this with friends who have knowledge of owl behaviour they explained that it could be a one-year-old bird, not mature enough to breed, living a bachelor life-style before it reaches maturity at two years. It could have been this owl that caused the demise of the afore-mentioned Collared Dove, and not a Sparrowhawk.

The garden is full of bird-song, including the songs of two newly arrived species of warbler. The sweet cascading song of the Willow Warbler can be heard everywhere. The song of the Blackcap is also heard, very similar to that of the somewhat less common Garden Warbler. As always, I have difficulty in identifying them by song alone.

The recent warm weather has encouraged Peacock and Small Tortoiseshell butterflies to appear. They will have spent the winter hibernating as adults. For the last few weeks there have been sightings of the three species of white butterflies and good numbers of Orange-tips. These latter insects will have spent the winter as pupae. Hopefully there will be a patch of fresh green nettle growth in a sunny position for the caterpillars of the Peacock and Small Tortoiseshell butterflies. I allow the growth of crucifers such as hedge-garlic and cuckooflower for the Green-veined White butterflies, the Small Whites and the Orange-tips. A pot of nasturtiums for the Large White would be appreciated. Even in the current green climate not many gardeners will grow cabbages especially for the benefit of the latter insect.

June

May was one of the worst I can remember. The weather has been mostly windy, damp and cool, and the newly unfurled fresh green leaves have taken a hammering, often ripped from their twigs. Nevertheless the inclement weather has not interfered with the nesting of garden birds. Three broods of Blue Tits and two of Great Tits are occupying boxes. This is the first year that two pairs of Great Tits are nesting. I find them to be more territorial than their smaller cousins. I noticed that one pair of Great Tits had constructed their nest with very little material, and in fact the eggs were resting on the bare wood of the base of the box. A friend who monitors a large number of boxes in a nearby forest has observed an increasing tendency for these tits to make very sparsely constructed nests. He thinks that this phenomenon is contributing to nesting failure, particularly during protracted periods of inclement weather. The other pair has made a nest of sorts, though nowhere near as elaborate as that made by the Blue Tits. The latter, when leaving their nest, cover their eggs with a feather duvet. This may be to keep the eggs warm but it is more likely that it is to make a would-be predator think there are no eggs present.

Several pairs of House Sparrows are nesting in the ivy on the side of the house. On checking one nest when the parent had left, to my astonishment it contained a clutch of seven eggs, one of which was hatching. I have never known a sparrow clutch that large. Even more astonishing, eleven days later the young had fledged! I would have thought with such a large brood there would have been a longer fledging period, not in fact a shorter one. Within a few feet there is a continuous supply of nuts, sunflower seeds and mixed cereals, which may have accelerated their development. There has been talk about a decline in House Sparrow numbers. I counted a maximum of twelve birds during a recent sparrow count. If I carried out the count today I would see over twice that number because of the number of fledglings in the garden. There are at least eight nests in the ivy and three pairs have laid in closed-fronted nest-boxes. The policy of providing food all year round and allowing tangled growth of climbers has paid off.

A few days ago I found a dead female Blackbird below a window. On the window was a ghost of the bird, the wing-feathers clearly visible,

Great Tit

marked by dust where it had struck the glass. I had left the room door open and the bird may have thought there was a clear passage through to where another window could be seen. It is a good idea to keep room doors shut to prevent birds from making this fatal mistake.

The remains of a pigeon were found beneath the cupressus where the owl roosts. The owl has been present for the last two months and each evening there is still the frantic chorus of alarm notes from the garden birds as the owl wakes up and gets ready for its night hunting. It still makes its wavering hoot in the middle of the day as if it wants people to be aware of its presence.

The bird-table continues to be an important source of food for the garden birds. One must not stop feeding at this time of year. The parents require more food to satisfy their hungry progeny. Thanks to regular feeding the density of bird life in the garden is much greater than it is in the surrounding environmentally impoverished countryside. I am always pleased when another species of bird visits the bird-table and yesterday a Magpie visited for the first time. I welcome this flamboyant member of the crow family, more so than its cousins, the rapacious crows and Rooks. They can clear the bird-table of food in seconds.

July

A few years ago visits of woodpeckers to most gardens would have been a very infrequent occurrence. Recently however there has been a considerable increase in the number of visits of these photogenic birds as they make use of the regular supply of nuts in tit-feeders. I have been fortunate this year to have a family of Great Spotted Woodpeckers making regular visits to the garden for food. I believe there are at least two young. One can feed itself while the other has to be fed by its parents. This species of bird is unusual in that the young are slightly more colourful than their parents. The young have a red crown, while the adult male has only a small red patch on its nape and the adult female has a purely black-and-white head.

The four pairs of House Sparrows nesting in the ivy on the house wall all have young, their second broods. A Robin has laid four eggs in a nest-box a short distance away from its first nest in a tangle of clematis. Robins are evidently not creatures of habit when it comes to nest sites. The Blackbirds and Song Thrushes could well be nesting for the third time and the garden is full of the raucous calls of their young.

I may be optimistic, but I feel garden wildlife is increasing, perhaps because more householders are regularly supplying food. One must continue to feed the birds through the summer months as their numbers are at a peak.

A few mornings ago I looked hopefully at my moth-trap, anticipating a good catch after one of the very few warm and calm nights we have had this season. I noticed that there seemed to be something of a disturbance in the trap. Was it caused by a swarm of Dark Arches or even an active Hawkmoth? No, it was a frantic Great Tit, which had entered the trap in search of easy pickings. Like a lobster in a lobster pot it had found it easy to get in but impossible to get out, but not before it had gorged itself on half of the moths, leaving just their wings. Fortunately I managed to identify most of the moths by examining their excised appendages, but I hope it is not another phenomenon starting to develop. Manufacturers may have to develop anti-tit barriers on moth-traps as they have anti-squirrel barriers on tit-feeders.

August
We have passed the peak of summer and the nights are beginning to draw in. Most of the songbirds have stopped singing as the time of finding a mate and establishing a territory has passed. The garden is full of birds, but the washed-out colours of the young Blue and Great Tits and the faded plumage of their parents give a general appearance of dullness. They are reducing the level of nuts in the feeders at a phenomenal rate. Larger birds, such as the Great Spotted Woodpeckers, have joined them. When these pied peckers are hammering at the feeders no other birds are there, but the House Sparrows wait underneath to pick up the fragments shaved off by their chisel-like beaks. Rooks and Jackdaws visit the table for the mixed seed but also try to get at the nuts in the feeders. They find it impossible to hang on the feeders but recently have found that they can unhook them from the table. When the feeders are on the ground they try to wrench off the caps and get at the nuts inside. I have had to make the cap more difficult to remove. The Rooks have also found that they can tip up the sunflower seed-dispenser, causing the seeds to slide out onto the ground. A Bank Vole exploits this situation! I had placed some large stones on the base of the table to anchor it down during windy weather. The Bank Vole has taken up temporary residence among the stones and when the sunflower seeds are tipped out, the opportunist rodent dashes out to grab one, taking it back into its refuge to devour it. It now has a nest composed entirely of sunflower husks!

One of the wild cherry trees has produced a good crop of fruit and the Blackbirds have been making a meal of them. There is a glut of raspberries and blackcurrants, possibly due to the damp weather. Curiously the birds have not decimated them this year.

I recently saw a flash of red in the large pond and discovered that

132

goldfish had survived there. It is over a year since the unwelcome visits of a Heron. I thought it had removed all the fish and for a whole year I had not been aware of any survivors. There were in fact six fish remaining. I tried feeding them, but they disappeared into the weeds if I made the slightest movement. They had become extremely shy. Does it mean that only the most secretive and shy fish have eluded the Heron's deadly bill, or have the survivors, as a result of their traumatic experience, become extremely nervous. If it is the latter, it is incredible that their modified behaviour should have continued for so long.

September

I don't think that many of us will regret the ending of summer 2002. Let us hope that we have a tranquil autumn after such a dull, damp and dismal season. I am fortunate that my property is on a slope and during the heavy storm of a few weeks ago the floodwaters raced down the drive, missing both house and garden. Not so lucky were several unfortunate householders in the village who suffered not only swamped gardens but also flooded homes.

In spite of the atrocious weather a few butterflies are visiting buddleia and other nectar-rich flowers. This year we have not been plagued by wasps or houseflies, though the small black garden ants decided to swarm during the brief hot spell we had a few days ago. During this period, a neighbour arrived at my door with a female House Sparrow in distress. The hot sun had melted the bitumen on his roof extension and the gooey material had oozed like lava into the gutter where the unfortunate bird had landed. The bird was in a terrible state. Among other injuries it had dislocated its legs in its struggles and it was completely covered in tar. We decided the kindest thing to do was to put it to sleep. There are occasions when a peaceful end is preferable to allowing an animal to stay alive in agony if it cannot be saved.

The Great Spotted Woodpeckers continue to visit the tit-feeders. They only arrive one at a time but I know that there is more than one bird, as their head plumage shows that an adult male, a female and a young bird are in attendance. When cutting back shrubs below a window I came across the decomposed remains of a woodpecker. It appeared to have killed itself by flying into the glass. It is unlikely that it was killed by concussion as the skull of this bird is especially reinforced to withstand the mind-numbing impact of bashing its beak like a pneumatic drill against a solid tree trunk. It must have broken its neck, since its muscles would not have been prepared for the impact.

Now that the birds have finished nesting it is time to inspect the nest-boxes and remove any debris, including unhatched eggs and the squashed corpses of dead nestlings, not an activity that I relish! This will remove any disease or parasites that would linger over winter and infest the nesting material next spring. Any suitably constructed boxes, which have not been occupied in the last two years, should be re-positioned, as their situation may not be to the liking of prospective builders. The feeders and bird-table should be cleaned and if possible re-sited to avoid a build-up of disease.

October

We have been enjoying a belated summer. With the exception of one or two days it has been consistently dry with frequent sunshine. The weather has been so amenable that a second flowering has taken place. The honeysuckle has had as many blooms as it had in mid-summer, dandelions and daisies are in flower and even the laburnum has an inflorescence or two! More butterflies have visited the garden in the last few days than in the whole of July.

I have said previously how, when I empty the moth-traps in the morning, a Robin is in attendance, ready to pick up a tasty Large Yellow Underwing or other nutritious Noctuid. The other morning as it was raining I was checking the moth trap in the conservatory instead of in the garden. The robin came in, in pursuit of moths yet to be released, and could not find its way out. Its panic before I could rescue it may in future discourage it from further trying to deplete my garden lepidopteran population.

We are reminded however that autumn is upon us with its shorter days and chilly nights. The first visual signs of the seasonal change in the wildlife garden include the birch leaves, changing to a pale gold, and the growth of fungi on the lawn and under the trees. The annual fairy-ring of mushrooms has again appeared in spite of near drought conditions.

November

The belated summer of September and early October is now a distant memory as we enter November. The garden is winding down for winter, most birds have stopped singing and those with any sense have already migrated south to sunnier climes. This time of the year however, is not the end, but only part of a cycle. Green shoots of snowdrops are already showing above ground and winter migrants have arrived from the far north.

The owl is back in the garden. The frantic alarm notes of the neighbourhood songbirds always advertise its presence. The other morning the loud clamour directed my attention to the almost bare branches of the nearby trees. I gazed in vain, looking for the characteristic familiar hump of a roosting owl. Then I saw it, perched on the top of the owl-box, about to enter it to roost through the day. I would like to think that it would decide to use the box for breeding in the spring.

The smaller birds are now visiting the bird-table and tit-feeders more frequently as the days get shorter, limiting the time available for foraging. I still get regular visits from Great Spotted Woodpeckers, and all four species of tits are regular attenders. They have to work for their supper by having to peck off small pieces of nut through a small mesh! Whole nuts placed on the bird-table will soon disappear, the main culprits being the Coal Tits. They fly to and fro carrying away nuts, only a few of which they will eat.

December

At the end of the year it is appropriate to pause and consider any changes that have taken place in the garden in the last twelve months. Though I have heard several Song Thrushes singing in the spring there has been little nesting activity; in contrast there have been numerous broods of Blackbirds reared. The colony of House Sparrows has increased to half-a-dozen breeding pairs. The authorities maintain that nationally there has been a significant decrease in the numbers of this familiar bird so I am pleased that I appear to be bucking the trend. This however is not an accident. When I moved into my house fifteen years ago, no sparrows bred. I have since planted ivy, honeysuckle, and Virginia creeper against the house walls and the building is now completely engulfed in their

135

triffid-like embrace. It is in this tangle that the sparrows have nested. Another factor is that wild bird food, a mixture of seeds and small-grained cereals, is available on the bird-table throughout the year. The other species to particularly benefit from my generosity is the Collared Dove, of which several pairs breed all the year round. All species of garden bird depend on food, shelter and cover for nesting, and if these requirements are satisfied they will flourish, as long as they and their fledglings are not predated by the neighbourhood cats.

Richard's articles were discontinued for several months during 2003 and 2004; these years have not been included in the account.

Long-tailed Fieldmouse

January

At 7 a.m. on the morning of 8th January the lights went out after a horrendous night of high winds and heavy rain. At first light I ventured outside to find a scene of destruction in the garden. The most serious consequence for me of the stormy night was the blocking of the drive by two large cupressus trees. They were too heavy to move on my own. However with the help of two neighbours, one equipped with suitable saws and also a dab hand with an axe, we managed to lop off the branches and drag the trunks to one side. It was only later that we realised the extent

137

of the flooding in Carlisle. We had got off very lightly in our slightly elevated location.

I have recently made a new pond for wildlife and have found that the pressure of ground water after all the recent rain has forced the plastic liner upwards. The natural water table has risen to the ground surface. Hopefully the liner will go back to its original bed as the garden dries out. As well as the toppled cupressus, a large apple tree has been toppled. It is not surprising that evergreens become uprooted in gales, because of the resistance of their leaves to the wind. It is less usual for leafless deciduous trees to be blown over. The apple tree was blown over because it has a mantle of ivy, the leaves of which caused resistance to the wind. I had allowed the ivy to grow in order to provide cover and nesting places for birds, as well as food. Woodpigeons particularly like to eat ivy berries. Actions carried out to make the garden more wildlife friendly have made it more prone to storm damage.

The weather has been extremely mild, encouraging snowdrops to flower much earlier than usual, at the beginning of January. Whether the storms are connected to our increasingly mild winters is a matter of opinion but as far as the garden is concerned autumn seems to run into spring.

February
For the three weeks following the high winds and heavy rain of early January there has been very little rain. The weather has been calm and mild, and on some days it has been quite spring like, encouraging a Song Thrush to make an attempt at singing on the morning of 27th January. Since then it has sung each morning and again in the afternoon as dusk approaches, causing a rival to start singing in opposition.

I have purchased a chainsaw to cut up the fallen trees and branches but decided to leave the inclining apple tree. It is resting on the adjoining hedge and a neighbouring tree. This tangle I will develop as a feature. The sawn branches and logs I have added to the woodpile previously built to shelter small mammals.

While working in the garden I noticed what I took to be a small grey ball rolling across the lawn. On closer inspection I found it to be a tiny shrew, its nose like a miniature elephant's trunk, but covered in sensitive hairs and quivering all the time. The shrew was about a quarter the size of a Fieldmouse or a Bank Vole and I took it to be a Pigmy Shrew. Mice and voles are rodents, but shrews are insectivores, feeding on worms and other invertebrates with their tiny sharp teeth. I released it where I had captured it, and it scuttled away none the worse for its encounter with me.

Prior to the storm I had begun to remove sections of ivy and Virginia creeper from the house walls, much to the relief of the window-cleaner who had had a problem finding the windows. The remains of several House Sparrows' nests were found. Since I encouraged creepers to grow on the walls several pairs of these gregarious birds have built their untidy nests in the tangled mixture of ivy, creeper and honeysuckle. I had waited until the end of the nesting season before I ripped off sections of creeper growth, to avoid causing disturbance. Likewise I wait until winter to cut the hedges. Nothing can be more harmful to garden birds than cutting hedges in the middle of the nesting season.

A few days ago I was entertained by the antics of at least a dozen Long-tailed Tits feeding in the apple trees. These tiny delicate tits are usually found in family parties at this time of year and follow each other in their relentless search for spiders and other hibernating insects. Their larger cousins, the Great Tits and Blue Tits, are still not visiting the bird-table as frequently as they usually do at this time of year. Can it be that they continue to find enough to eat in the fields and hedgerows? Food should still be put out on the bird table for when last year's available food has been eaten there is still a long wait before the coming spring's supply is on line.

March

As I dug over my garden a few days ago a Robin mistook me for a pig, not because of my appearance, I hope, but because of what I was doing. In the ancient European wildwood, Robins followed the wild boars in order to access worms and other invertebrates unearthed by rooting snouts. To this day the local Robin arrives to obtain prey, not uprooted by a snout, but by the spade of the gardener.

On a mild day in February I was pleased to see a pair of frogs in the pond, the smaller male mounted on the back of the female. I was hoping that they were beginning to spawn, but the wind then changed to the east and the cold winds cooled the ardour of these amorous amphibians. I have not seen a frog since. Recently a neighbour found the remains of frogs and ornamental fish around her pond. I also heard of large pond fish being killed by an Otter elsewhere in the neighbourhood. It is easy to confuse the actions of Mink, Herons or even cats with those of an Otter. However, in spite of the damage they can cause, it is exciting that such a charismatic mammal is increasing in number in our area.

Some weeks ago I ordered two owl boxes from a catalogue circulated with a local conservation magazine. When they arrived they were in fact Little Owl boxes, much too small for any other type of owl. I decided to keep them and use them as Starling boxes. I covered up the open front of one with a piece of wood, after making a Starling sized nest hole in it. Soon a pair of Starlings was seen popping in and out. Two days later they began to take building material into the box. This was very early, as the huge Starling roosts had not at that time dispersed. Perhaps most of these roosting birds are foreigners from Scandinavia, delaying returning to their homelands because of their cold winters.

April

On the last day of March a Robin flew out of a tiny wicker roosting-chamber placed on a tree close beside the drive. I would never have expected a bird to nest in such a place. Crammed inside in the restricted space was a nest containing one egg. It's the first time this has occurred in the garden in such a site. It is also very early. On that same early date a Blackbirds' nest containing three eggs was found.

Some weeks ago I converted two old music-centre speakers into nests. After removing the front covers, two holes were exposed on each speaker. The upper smaller hole was just the right size for a Starling to access. The lower hole was larger and could be used as an inspection hatch. A thin square of plywood was placed over this hole, kept in place by two screws in slots. On 1st April Starlings adopted both of these boxes and the proud new occupants were carrying in long lengths of grasses to make their nests.

On inspecting the moth-trap one morning I was surprised to find a female Palmate Newt hiding underneath it. The Palmate Newt is slightly smaller than the Common or Smooth Newt. The male has dark webbing between the toes of its rear legs and a hair-like extension to its tail. The female Common and Palmate Newts are more difficult to tell apart, but the Palmate has fewer freckles under its chin than the Common Newt. A few Great Crested Newts visit the large pond to breed. Both frogs and toads are spawning. The first frog-spawn was late this year, on 22nd March and the first toad-spawn was seen on the same date. Usually toads spawn a week or so after frogs but the fickle weather, cold winds followed quickly by quite warm weather, has telescoped their spawning times. This spring there have been more spawning toads than frogs. There also appears to have been an identity crisis with amphibians of one species trying to clasp individuals of the other for breeding purposes! One eager frog had clasped a mating pair of toads. After a couple of days I decided to interfere and prised off the amorous frog, only for it to repeat its

Palmate Newt

unacceptable act some time later.

The nesting season is getting under way with the arrival of summer migrants from the south. I have heard the song of the Chiffchaff, a repetitive '*chiff-chaff chiff-chaff*', from which sound it obviously gets its name. A fortnight later the sweet cascading song of the Willow Warbler was heard again.

A welcome garden visitor on 19th March was a Peacock butterfly, out of hibernation on the first warm day of spring. One less welcome visitor was a Heron, which flew from the ponds when I looked out first thing in the morning. I hope it has not caught any of the fish or, equally important, any of the amphibians.

May

Towards the end of April two important events took place on the same day. Firstly I fell off a ladder while inspecting an owl-box. Warning! Never rest your ladder by its top rung on a curved tree trunk, for it will twist and unbalance you. On staggering into the house I was at least partly compensated for the pain in my wrenched foot by the sight of a Comma butterfly, the first ever in my garden. I have commented on the northward movement of this colourful insect and had become increasingly impatient to obtain my first home sighting. Look out for a butterfly which resembles the much more common Small Tortoiseshell, but which has ragged edges to the wings. The 'comma' is a white mark on the underside of the rear wings, just like the punctuation mark.

There have never been so many newts, both Common and Palmate, in the ponds as there are this spring! Other local naturalists have made the same observation. There have been several clumps of frog-spawn and strings of toad-spawn. The eggs have hatched but few tadpoles are left, in all probability predated by the newts.

The nesting season proceeds in full swing. Two Robins' nests were built only thirty yards from each other, each with five eggs. This I found surprising as Robins are territorial and I would have thought that the first Robins to nest would not allow the second pair to build. Unfortunately the second nest, in a tiny open-fronted box, was destroyed, probably by a cat, as was a nearby Blackbirds' nest. Cats are a problem at this time of the year when young fledglings leave the nest but are unable to fly properly.

A Blackbird is nesting three feet from my front door. It had laid one egg before I realised it was there. When it completed its clutch of four it remained sitting tight, even if I was only two feet away from it. It was obviously familiar with me moving about. In contrast, a Starling nesting a few feet away on the other side of the door was extremely timid, leaving the box at the slightest sound. Even touching the door handle on the inside caused it to leave its nest. It behaved like this right up to the hatching of two of its four eggs. The third egg hatched twelve hours later and the fourth over a day later. The youngster was hardly half the size of its siblings. I was pleased that all hatched successfully in spite of the constant interruptions to brooding. On 23rd April the first egg was laid in the Great Tits' nest-box. The parents had lined the nest with white hair that had been cut from my head and thrown in the garden! On 27th April there was a first egg in the Blue Tit box, lying hidden in its soft bed of feathers, without a trace of my hair!

The nest-boxes sent to me under the false premise of being owl boxes have at least been of use. Having boxed in the fronts and made a Starling-sized hole in the wood each is now occupied by a pair of Starlings, brooding full clutches of eggs.

June

I have just got back from a holiday in rural France. I was greatly impressed with the wildflower meadows and their associated butterflies, reminiscent of the countryside I remember as a child. The situation in our countryside, where for a long time wildlife has had little consideration, is thankfully to some extent being reversed. We should continue to garden for wildlife in order to retain reservoirs of animals and plants. From our gardens they will spread out into the surrounding farmland as it gradually becomes more wildlife-friendly.

While I was away, two nests of Great Tits and one brood of Blue Tits fledged. Sadly however in each box the carcass of at least one chick re-mained. They could have died because the cool inclement weather had caused a lack of caterpillars and aphids. One hopes they had not been poisoned by the use of pesticides applied in an attempt to eradicate greenfly. At this time of year, particularly when it is damp, small grey slugs are a nuisance, coming out at night to ravage the newly planted border annuals. One can unthinkingly turn to slug-pellets, which are extremely efficient in removing them. Sadly Hedgehogs and Song Thrushes are also killed, as they eat the dead slugs contaminated with metaldehyde.

Before I went away a thrush was nesting in an ivy-covered apple tree just outside the conservatory window. I did not disturb it by looking for the nest but saw the parents taking in food. When I returned from holiday I was surprised to see the same activity at that nest. On investigation I found the nest with three recently hatched young and one chipping egg, a second clutch. I would not have looked in if I had known, but did not expect the thrush to have laid again. I have usually found that thrushes build a new nest for a new clutch. The young have fledged from the Blackbirds' nest by the front door and four more eggs have been laid in the same nest. Again I have found that Blackbirds usually build a new nest – even if it is on top of the old one. Is this re-use of a nest a trend, perhaps due to a shortage of building sites?

A Blue Tit has built a nest and laid six eggs in one of the starling boxes. The entrance hole was so big that the tiny tits could almost fly freely through the hole. This tit was a late nester. Perhaps her first attempt at nesting had failed, but why choose such a large box? There are plenty of smaller boxes in the garden.

It has been a rather cool and unsettled spring and early summer with particularly cold nights, not conducive to ample catches of moths in the garden moth-trap. Towards the end of May there was a mild night and several species of moth were captured, including the impressive Poplar Hawkmoth and the distinctive Buff-tip, which resembles a broken twig. The most interesting feature of the catch was seven large cockchafers or May Bugs. These night flying beetles are large, heavy and black, covered with short grey hair and have a spiked tip to their abdomen. Their young are crescent shaped maggots that feed destructively on the roots of grasses, cereals and young trees. After pupation the adults emerge in the October of their third summer but remain dormant until the following May, when they leave the ground and fly, adding to the interesting diversity of wildlife in our gardens.

The two broods of young Starlings in the 'owl' boxes have fledged.

Both they and their parents are producing raucous calls reminiscent of a jay rather than the usual twittering emitted for most of the year.

July

Recently I heard on the radio a discussion concerning the scarcity of hedgehogs in gardens. Coincidentally I also have been concerned about the lack of these insectivores in the garden. Not only have I not seen one this year, but I have not found their characteristic droppings on the lawn.

Perhaps in some compensation for the absence of the prickly urchin I have been entertained by the antics of a colony of Bank Voles that live at the base of an ivy-covered apple tree only a few feet from the bird-table just outside the conservatory door. Usually at dusk, but sometimes in broad daylight, these charming little rodents scurry from the safety of their lair, as if on tiny wheels, and snatch a nut fallen from the table. If there is no food on the ground they climb up the post onto the table and sometimes even hang on the nut-feeders. The tits show little concern at their presence.

A Song Thrush has laid a second clutch of eggs in a nest in the above-mentioned apple tree. Eleven days after the eggs had hatched I found a nestling thrush on the ground under the tree. Its feathers were not developed enough for it to have left the nest naturally. Young thrushes are normally two or three days older before they fledge. It is likely that the nest had been predated by a Magpie or a cat. Its siblings had been taken, most likely eaten. I placed the youngster back in the nest and was pleased to see that its parents were feeding it. It fledged successfully some days later. If you find a young bird which has obviously fledged, but appears to be abandoned, do not move it or take it away, as its parents will be around, ready to feed it when you leave. However if it is in immediate danger, such as on a road, move it to a place of safety close by.

The other night, after dark, I went out to the pond with a powerful torch and shone it in the water. As well as the adult newts that I usually see in daylight, there were large numbers of immature part-grown newts. They had emerged from the cover of the waterweed and were feeding on a dense swarm of tiny animals, including *Cyclops* and *Daphnia* (water-fleas). There were no frog or toad tadpoles – the huge numbers of adult newts will probably have eaten them.

August

As we move through the summer the numbers and variety of moths in the garden increases. One night recently I caught thirty-one species of macro (large) moth. As usual a Robin follows me to devour moths released after identification! No matter how carefully I hide them in the bushes, the observant redbreast finds some of the released insects and has them for its breakfast. This has been happening in my garden for some years now. However a few weeks ago a House Sparrow muscled in and took over from the Robin. On occasion I have seen it fly after a released moth and capture it as if it were a Flycatcher.

Some days ago, while standing on top of a ladder removing some overgrown ivy from the top of the house wall, I was suddenly surrounded by a swarm of wasps. I had disturbed their nest under the eaves. I beat a hasty retreat down the ladder! The wasps seemed smaller than ordinary wasps, and I assumed they were Tree Wasps. They were not doing me any harm and they do a lot of good in the garden, killing numerous insect pests, so I decided to leave the nest alone.

There has been a much less welcome visitor to the garden recently! I have previously written about a colony of Bank Voles that visit my bird-table from their home in the ivy-covered base of a nearby tree. I had not seen these charming little rodents for a few days but recently I saw a large face peering from the tree base at the food on the bird-table. It remained still for a minute or so, and then the creature emerged. It was a rat! I have stopped putting food on the table and I have not seen it again, thank goodness, but neither have I seen the voles.

I have been reclaiming part of my garden from the wilderness that it has developed into during the last few years. The main problem has been getting rid of horsetails, tiresome invasive weeds, deep rooted and hollow stemmed. Without using herbicides it is a near impossible task. The evil-looking mat of roots defies complete removal, particularly in the rockery.

Recently I had the pleasure of wandering around gardens open to the public in village garden trails. As well as being humbled by the sheer beauty and the obvious hard work required to produce such a high standard, I was also gratified to see that parts of several gardens were also designed with wildlife in mind. Of particular note were several extremely beautiful wildflower meadows in some of the larger gardens.

September *(1)*

Perhaps as a result of the prolonged period of hot, dry weather followed by a few cool days, some of the trees think it is autumn already. Even before July had ended the leaves on the top of a sycamore tree turned gold. By mid-August the silver birch leaves had also turned pale gold and covered the car parked underneath like confetti. With the return to more typical showery weather this race into autumn may slow down.

I have recently been fascinated by the behaviour of five Collared Doves. Two pairs were mating close to each other while a fifth bird looked on. It is a delicate affair, in contrast to the wing bashing of Woodpigeons. One pair then sat on the edge of the birdbath in steady rain. It was hot and humid and one of them raised a wing, as if enjoying the sensuous sensation of rain on its near-naked breast.

The garden has been visited on two separate occasions by a Comma butterfly. This is particularly welcome, as it has only recently established itself in the north of Cumbria. Another butterfly came to the garden for the first time recently. A Small Copper, its name appropriately describing its size and colour, settled briefly on a stone near where I was working. Its larval food plant is sorrel, a humble weed that could well be allowed to grow in a less prominent part of a garden.

September *(2)*

A couple of weeks ago my attention was drawn to the sight of a small brightly coloured insect, apparently inspecting the base of the wall. I had never seen such an animal before and on searching in various books was able to identify it as a Ruby-tailed Wasp. This brilliant blue-green and crimson wasp *(Chrysis)* is a nest-parasite and lays its eggs in the nesting burrows of other solitary wasps and bees. Its larvae not only devour the food-store provided by the original owner of the nest, but the young bee or wasp larva as well. Another name for this insect is the Cuckoo-wasp. *Chrysis ignita* is the most common Ruby-tailed Wasp, usually seen flying around walls and fences in warm weather. It has a metallic red abdomen and greenish-blue head and thorax. It has lost the ability to sting, and rolls up into a ball when threatened. The female can be seen inspecting holes and cracks in walls. If a bee or wasp occupies a hole the female Cuckoo-wasp slips inside and lays her own eggs there, where they hatch in a week. If more than one has been laid the first one to hatch eats the rest. The larva waits in the hole for the rightful owner to become fully grown and then feeds on it until fully grown itself. The plump larva then spins a cocoon to over-winter. It pupates in spring and emerges as an adult in June. A fascinating, if somewhat gruesome, life history.

Another insect that drew my attention about the same time was a large dragonfly with lime-green markings on its thorax and down its abdomen. It was a female Southern Hawker dragonfly, an insect that has become increasingly common around garden ponds in our area during the last decade or so. It kept settling on mossy stones and appeared to be trying to lay eggs. During this process I examined it closely and even took macro-photos of it with my digital camera but I saw no eggs. At no time did it attempt to lay in the water.

This is the time of year when I can get requests to identify a particular beast, sometimes described as a legless lizard, the larva of an Elephant Hawkmoth. Recently a gentleman called at my house with such a specimen. The adult moth is a large beautiful insect, its wings suffused with pink, similar in colour to the flowers of its food plants, namely bogbean, rosebay willowherb and fuchsia.

A much less welcome visitor entered my garden on 11th September. On examining my two small ponds I noticed that the pots on the margins had been knocked over and the water lilies had all but been uprooted. I later found that all the fish had been taken from one pond and only two were left in the other. There appeared to be little disturbance in the large pond, kept purely as a wildlife pond. A Mink had visited the garden. The ponds are protected from Herons, and in any case a Heron would not have left so much damage. Several others in the village have had similar experiences. One garden pond has been visited more than once. I have to be philosophical. I will not replace the ornamental fish and will leave the smaller ponds as wildlife ponds. Sadly the mink did return some nights later and took the remaining fish.

Redwings

October

At the end of October we are entering the dark time of the year when nature slows down for winter. I heard the characteristic *'see-ih'* sound of Redwings as they passed over in the darkness, and on the following day a small party descended on the garden to feed on the hawthorn berries. The Redwing is similar in size to a Song Thrush but can be distinguished by its prominent white eye-stripe and red flashes on its flank and under its wings. Their arrival was followed a few days later by their larger and much more garrulous cousins, the Fieldfares. These Blackbird-sized thrushes can be identified by a blue-grey head, nape and rump, a chestnut back, dark tail and speckled brown breast. Both these winter visitors are in competition with our resident thrushes for the dwindling supply of fruit and berries.

Insects, such as Small Tortoiseshells and Peacock Butterflies might move indoors at this time of year. One can sometimes find them hibernating behind the curtains. More unwelcome prospective hibernators are queen wasps preparing to hide away, to start a new nest in the spring. I gently encouraged one out of the house a few days ago.

November

When looking out of my window on the afternoon of 6th November, there was movement at the edge of my field of vision. Something glided across the garden and settled in the boundary hedge. From the cacophony of small bird alarm notes I assumed it to be an owl. I walked down to the hedge and through the foliage did in fact see an owl fly off into the adjoining field. The chorus of bird alarms faded away. Some time later on returning to the hedge I saw a Tawny Owl standing in clear view on the bare branch of an ash tree. Strangely there were no small birds calling! The owl watched me with its beautiful dark eyes, its neck swivelling around as if on ball-bearings. It sat watching me for so long that I tired and left. I have never before seen an owl stay so long in an exposed position in broad daylight. One explanation could be that the noise and flashing lights of Bonfire Night had disturbed it. We are often concerned about the panic fireworks can cause to domestic pets, but overlook how this disturbance might affect the wild animals and birds that live in our gardens. This owl has taken up residence in the high hedge and at the onset of dusk the alarm notes of the garden birds advertise its presence.

Until the middle of November the weather was extremely mild. Buttercups and dandelions have been flowering in the hedgerows and I have seen both Peacock and Red Admiral butterflies sunning themselves. Peacocks should have been hibernating, along with Small Tortoiseshell butterflies. The status of the Red Admiral as a hibernator is still debatable. Some years ago it was considered to be only a migrant and that it did not hibernate in Britain. Recently however some individuals have been found to spend the whole winter here, though usually in the south.

There has been little activity at the bird-table for the last few weeks because of the abundance of wild food. Haws, elderberries and grass-seeds are still plentiful in the countryside. When autumn progresses into winter the bird-table will become much busier as the wild harvest runs out. Then is the time to ensure that a ready supply of food is provided for garden birds. Any windfall apples should be left on the ground, or at least kept on one side to be placed on the lawn at a later time. Blackbirds and thrushes will feed on them. It is also helpful to plant shrubs such as hawthorn to provide berries in the future.

December

There is not a lot going for the month of December in the garden. It can be cold, damp and dark, but its saving grace is that by the end of the month the days start to get longer. Activity in the garden is at its lowest ebb but the gloom and damp was brightened the other day by the activities of two tiny birds restlessly searching the bark on the apple trees for the tiniest of prey, perhaps spiders or hibernating flies. The band of light gold over their heads identified them as Goldcrests, our smallest resident bird.

Sunday 11th December was an unusually beautiful day and a Peacock butterfly was sunning itself, enticed out of hibernation by the mild weather. Sadly its activity will use up precious energy resources and as there are few nectar-laden flowers about to refuel it, its chances of surviving the winter are remote. The danger for hibernating creatures is not the cold, but mild spells, which cause them to become active and use up their energy resources.

Another sight to lighten the heart on that day was a beautiful spray of gorse flowers. This bush can break into bloom in any month of the year, hence the old saying 'when gorse is out of flower, kissing is out of fashion'.

As the hedgerow fruits and berries become depleted so the garden birds become more dependent on our generosity in supplying them with food. During the last week or so I have frequently had to replenish the tit-feeders with nuts and to scatter more wild birdseed on the bird-table. Any remaining windfall apples should be left for our resident Blackbirds and winter visitors such as Fieldfares from Scandinavia.

Flag-iris

January

At last, thank goodness, Christmas and the New Year are behind us. The darkest time of the year has passed and even though the coldest period of the winter may be still to come, the garden is showing signs that spring may not be too far ahead. The winter jasmine has finished flowering, and sweet-smelling Winter-sweet has taken over. The green shoots of snowdrops, daffodils, crocus and even the later flowering bluebells are beginning to push through the mat of dead leaves. Tiny white 'rabbit-tails' are beginning to show on the willow and catkins of 'lambs'-tails' are showing on the hazel.

I was watching the behaviour of two male Blackbirds yesterday, both in jet-black glossy breeding plumage, contrasting with their lemon-yellow bills. They were challenging each other, at the first stage of establishing nesting territories, a sure sign that spring, though distant, is on the way.

At this time of year it is easy to watch birds in the garden. The summer visitors are absent. The resident birds can be easily identified as they can be seen in full view on the tit-feeders and bird-table and there is little leaf cover for them to skulk behind. Ideally the bird-table should be situated in the field of view from a large window where one can sit in a comfortable chair with a pair of binoculars.

Re-stocking the bird table with seed can keep one busy at this time of year. If I placed wild-bird seed on the bird-table in the late afternoon I was finding that the table was bare by the morning. I realised that at first light a gang of Rooks from the nearby rookery, along with a pair of Jackdaws and the odd crow, had hoovered up everything. These wary corvids prefer the quiet of early morning for their feast. When the small garden birds arrive there was nothing left. I find it much better to place the food out about mid-morning when the finches and tits are around. Their larger cousins keep clear whilst there is more human activity about.

February

We have been let off gently up to now this winter with little wind or rain and no snow. I have been out in the garden working in near spring-like conditions, trying to clear twenty years of accumulated debris. I had allowed it to accrue partly because it would provide shelter for small animals and minibeasts, and also because I do not like bonfires, which cause air pollution. As the heap settled, it did not produce a rash of green vegetation as I had hoped. This was probably because the garden clippings were resting on a base of logs, which prevented weeds from becoming rooted. In addition the top layer of branches was too light to break down into a compact loam. I decided to tackle the problem by removing the logs and branches and stacking them separately. The remaining woody debris was raked up leaving a loam rich in humus. Lately the disposal of unwanted garden debris has been made easier by the provision of wheelie-bins. I have purchased a second bin and wait impatiently for both of them to be emptied so that I can quickly refill them.

The countdown to spring has begun. On 16th January snowdrops were flowering and on the same day a pair of Great Tits was inspecting a nest-box. On 26th January there was a short burst of song from a Song Thrush. Since then other tits have been popping in and out of boxes and Dunnocks and Robins are singing vigorously. This slow movement into spring reminds me of the film *Journey into Spring* that I saw about fifty years ago, well before the current plethora of natural history films seen nightly on television. It was filmed in Selbourne, the Hampshire village where Gilbert White, one of the first English naturalists, lived in the eighteenth century. He recorded every tiny natural event that took place in and around his village. The film used locations around Selbourne that were mentioned in his book, *The Natural History of Selbourne*. Some years later I showed this film to a class of African students. They were surprised and amused to see the thatched roofs of the village cottages, so similar to those of their own huts.

March

I have recently been visiting my hometown of Beverley. I can remember when I was a small boy playing on The Westwood, a square mile of common land where there were three ponds. They were called respectively Tadpole Pond, Newt Pond and Red Rudd (stickleback) Pond. It was from this experience that I developed my interest in nature. Today there are no ponds on The Westwood. They have been filled in, why I do not know. Small boys today are denied this enjoyment and learning experience. A garden is not a wildlife garden without a pond, and with spring on the way, now is the time to think about making one. Ponds are very important as reservoirs of wildlife.

There has been an amazing increase in the number of Buzzards locally. They are now often seen flying over the garden and perching on posts around the village. In contrast there has been a noticeable absence of Rooks in the garden recently, even though I have put suitable kitchen scraps out for them. At the other end of the village is a rookery and at this time of the year it should be alive with cawing corvids, but it is very quiet, with hardly a Rook present. I wonder what has happened! I like Rooks to visit the garden, along with their cousins the Carrion Crows, to clean up dinner leftovers. Some people have difficulty telling these two species apart. Rooks are glossy with shaggy 'trousers' and a bare pale patch at the base of the beak. Crows are sooty with a neater shape and a feathered beak. Crows croak and Rooks caw.

April

I have been watching a Robin carrying dead leaves to its half-built nest in an ivy-covered tree trunk, whilst another is building in a mossy bank. Perhaps the earliest bird to nest is a Song Thrush. It carries muddy weeds from the edge of the pond. A Blackbird is building in the cupressus hedge. Both Woodpigeons and Collared Doves are carrying fine twigs to their nest sites.

More birds have returned to the bird-table, with Greenfinches and the occasional Siskin feeding. The Robin, which had at first made tentative attempts at hanging on the feeders, is now feeding confidently all the time in this manner. The Coal Tits are back, each one carrying a nut away from the feeder to eat later. The garden is also graced by a pair of Pheasants, the cock pacing proudly to the base of the table to pick up the fallen grains. A Magpie has been calling from the high hedge during the last few days. Hopefully it will construct its roofed fortress of thorn in the top branches. An owl emerges each night at dusk to the sound of loud warning calls from all the garden songbirds.

A week ago I noticed a small dark fish in the small pond that had been cleaned out by the Heron. On closer inspection I found at least thirteen young fish. They were goldfish, but had not as yet acquired their gold colour, which happens as they mature. They must have hatched from eggs laid by the original goldfish before they were predated. I have removed the toad-spawn from this pond and placed it in the large pond. I hope both the toad tadpoles and the baby goldfish will survive. I heard a Chiffchaff singing in the village yesterday, the first of the summer migrants, and am now waiting for the first Swallow to fly over the garden.

May

Spring is very late this year, the hedges only recently becoming green and the trees not yet fully in leaf as we move into May. Three species of tit are sitting on eggs in boxes in the garden. Two pairs of Great Tits and a pair of Blue Tits have been sitting for some days, but I have been

Coal Tit

particularly excited by the nesting of a pair of Coal Tits. This is the first time in twenty years that a pair of these tiny birds has decided to use one of my nest-boxes for breeding. It was on 9th April that a Coal Tit was seen carrying material into a box which, to judge from the literature, was sited in an unsuitable position. It was placed against the trunk of an apple tree but surrounded by a tangle of branches and twigs. They usually nest low down, often amongst tree roots. The first egg was laid on 19th April and there were nine eggs six days later. The Coal Tit is the smallest of our resident tits and can be recognised by its glossy blue-black head and the white flash on the nape.

Outside the conservatory window is the apple tree wrapped round with a heavy shawl of ivy. Some weeks ago I noticed a Robin flying in and out carrying building material. For a week or so Robins were carrying tiny insects into the tree, and then latterly caterpillars and small worms. I had a quick look but could not locate the nest among the ivy jungle. I could have found it by diligently searching, but that is not recommended as it may cause the parents distress and even make them desert. A week ago Robins were again carrying building material into the ivy, but this time to a nest lower down, where to date they have laid three eggs. They have built a second nest whilst they appear to be still feeding an earlier brood. Though all Robins look the same I am certain it cannot be another pair as Robins are strictly territorial and the resident pair would not allow another pair to build in their territory. It is important not to disturb nesting birds and it is beneficial to allow ivy to form a thick covering round trunks of trees as cover for nesting birds and other wildlife.

On the occasional warm days butterflies have visited the garden, including Green-veined Whites, the Small Tortoiseshell and Peacock butterflies, which have hibernated as adults. I was excited to see on 28th April, in warm sunshine, a rather faded Comma butterfly, also woken from hibernation, resting in the tree where the Coal Tit was nesting. This is only the third one seen in my garden. It nearly ended up in the beak of one of the Coal Tits.

June

Some weeks ago I was hoping for rain. I had planted new shrubs on land that had been cleared of piled up branches. The soil was bone dry underneath. Since then however we have had more than enough rain and until recently the weather has continued to be cool. Nesting birds have been affected in various ways. The Blackbirds and thrushes have healthy youngsters, as there has been a plentiful supply of worms. The Robins are also benefiting. Their large brood of six active nestlings looks bizarre, with black tufts of down on their heads. The Blue Tits have only three nestlings. One parent stays brooding to keep the young warm. There is perhaps a shortage of food. A pair of Great Tits has only one youngster in the nest, which it is sharing with the corpses of two siblings. A few feet away there is a scattering of Great Tit feathers, perhaps advertising the demise of a parent. Only four young hatched from the six eggs in the other Great Tit nest-box. They seemed to be growing and healthy, though one of the parents spent a long time brooding. Later they all died, again perhaps due to the cold weather. The Coal Tit brood has done very well. Eight healthy nestlings fledged successfully.

A couple of months ago I found that a cock Wren had built one of its several nests only a foot away from the basement door. Several weeks later I found a lining had been added to the nest. The hen chose to lay her six eggs in this nest, all of which have hatched. Tucked behind a sprig of ivy on the house wall a female Chaffinch is sitting on a beautiful nest made of moss and lined with feathers. She laid five eggs and the nestlings are ready to leave home.

I have arranged for my high hedge to be cut down to half its height for safety reasons, but am delaying the operation to allow a Collared Dove and a Woodpigeon to finish nesting. I am always interested to watch the behaviour of Woodpigeons. Usually they waddle about the garden or demonstrate amorous actions with their partner on a tree branch with loud wing clapping. The other day however I saw what I thought was such behaviour develop into a sparring match and I realised they were birds from different pairs fighting. There were two pairs in the garden, one pair nesting in the cupressus hedge and the other in a tree near the gate. They are obviously to some extent territorial.

On 2nd June my attention was drawn to a blue butterfly flying at head height among the shrubs. The silvery tone to the blue colour of its wings and the nature of its flight identified it as a Holly Blue, another first for the garden. This occasional visitor to our gardens lays its eggs on holly flowers. In the south it has a second generation later in the summer, when ivy flowers are its food plant. Recently in the Carlisle area, Holly Blues have been seen later in the year. They must have successfully completed a second generation. A silvery-blue butterfly seen flying quite high in spring is likely to be a Holly Blue. The Common Blue flies at a much lower height.

July
At last, in late June, after a cool spring and early summer, we have been blessed with periods of warm sunny weather. More important to a moth enthusiast is that we have had some warm nights. The result of this has been an increase in both variety and number of moths caught. On some

mornings I have found as many as a hundred moths of some twenty-five species. Some of them are surprisingly colourful. The Garden Tiger moth is perhaps the most striking with its strong patterning and bright colouring. I have caught several of these handsome moths in the last few nights, which is gratifying as their numbers are falling throughout the country. I have also caught a Swallow-tailed Moth, the size of a Small White butterfly, lemon coloured with swallowtail-shaped wings.

Returning from two weeks holiday all the birds nests were empty. Hopefully the nestlings had fledged successfully. The garden is full of young birds. Some of them are recently fledged Blackbirds and thrushes, which as yet cannot fly properly and are easy prey for cats. Their strident chortles are not a sound of distress but a communication call for their parents, which will not be far away. These young birds have not been deserted. They should be left well alone for their parents to feed them. Fledgling tits appear to be quite efficient fliers when they leave their nest-boxes. All young birds are on a steep learning curve and crash into objects. The other day I picked up a stunned young Greenfinch from under the conservatory window. I brought it inside and left it alone. After about an hour it flew away through the open door. Left outside it might have become a meal for a cat.

Whilst watching a parent Song Thrush feeding its recently fledged youngster I realised that it was collecting small slugs from the leaf litter. Every time it found one it spent some time wiping it on the ground, obviously attempting to remove the slime before feeding it to its young.

I recently introduced some young sticklebacks into the small pond. I was beginning to despair that there were none left in our area, so I am pleased that they are still to be found. Hopefully they will grow and breed next year. Surely visiting Mink and Herons will find them too small and unpalatable.

August
We are currently in the grip of a protracted hot dry spell. Thrushes, Blackbirds and Robins, still with young to feed, are in quite serious trouble. Cherries were stripped from the trees as soon as they were ripe. A Blackbird has even joined a Robin and a House Sparrow in their attempts to gain a meagre morsel of moth as I release the catch from the

Long-tailed Tits

moth-trap in the morning.

I have had to rise as early as 5.15 a.m. to empty the moth-trap in order to avoid its contents being frizzled alive in the hot morning sun. As is to be expected in this hot humid weather the catch has consisted of hundreds of specimens of many species. The peak was one night when there were forty-three species, with thirteen new ones for the year. The most numerous were the Large Yellow Underwings, with seventy-four individuals.

Last year I moved two buddleia bushes from the lawn, where they had not flourished, to a dry and inhospitable raised rocky area with little soil. In spite of, or perhaps even because of, the drought they have flourished and have produced heavy panicles of sweet-smelling flowers. They have attracted quite a variety of butterflies, including Red Admirals, Small Tortoiseshells, Peacocks and recently a Painted Lady. The hot sun is causing the flower panicles to be quickly spent. I cut off the dead flowers, encouraging more to develop.

The apple trees are plagued with woolly aphids. They hide in what looks like cotton wool smeared on the broken bark. Some days ago a family party of Long-tailed Tits was passing through and on their way fed on these tiny insects. They are continuously on the move so unfortunately did not stay long enough to complete their task.

September *(1)*

After the hot, dry and sunny period, the garden has lately experienced weather more typical of an English summer. I would have liked more rainfall, as deep down the soil is still quite dry. There has been some heavy prolonged rain around us. A village only a couple of miles away has had continuous rain while we only had a dampening of the garden. The trees and herbaceous plants have stopped wilting and the birds have been able to access earthworms. A godsend for the Blackbirds has been the ripening of the early-fruiting apples and the garden is littered with the shells of these fruit. Eager beaks have removed the soft flesh, leaving the skins.

Some weeks ago there was a loud bang on the conservatory window and on looking out I saw what I thought was a female Chaffinch lying dead under the window. A minute later I saw a cock Bullfinch flitting around the bushes and I wondered where its mate was, as in my experience Bullfinches are usually seen in pairs. When I went to pick up the dead finch my query was answered. Its black tail feathers and white rump identified it as a female Bullfinch. Later that afternoon a Greenfinch flew into the window, but was only slightly stunned and flew away. I resolved to make amends and bought some cut out shapes of predatory birds for sticking to windows. Hopefully they will frighten any garden birds away from the windows. So far they seem to be effective. I also bought a three-in-one House Sparrow nest-box, a terrace for sparrows. It will be interesting to see if this will encourage more than one pair of these supposedly social birds to nest.

I can tell the progress of the seasons by examining the contents of the moth-trap. For the last week or two I have been catching Canary-shouldered Thorns and Sallow moths. Sadly they are harbingers of the approach of autumn. I caught an unusually small grey Silver-Y moth and while trying to box it, to examine it more closely, it escaped. I followed it with my eyes to recapture it when it settled. However it was intercepted and swallowed by the ever-present Robin.

A number of brightly coloured, predominantly yellow, caterpillars are feeding on the nasturtiums, the larvae of the Large White butterfly. Far from killing these so called pests, I leave them alone, hoping that they will pupate and emerge as adults. These beautiful butterflies seem to be less common than they used to be. The buddleia has been covered with butterflies, including many Small Whites. The beauty of butterflies can only be enjoyed if we allow caterpillars to cause some damage to our garden plants.

September *(2)*
The latter part of September has been unseasonably warm. The Victoria plum tree has been so overloaded with fruit that the main branch has been ripped away from its trunk with the weight of plums. In spite of the glut of rotting apples and fallen plums there has been little nuisance from wasps.

There are numbers of Red Admiral and Small Tortoiseshell butterflies still gliding about the garden. Until recently there were also plenty of Painted Lady and Peacock butterflies accompanying them on the buddleia. I had left a pile of early-ripening apples for the birds. The fruit quickly rotted and soon attracted a considerable number of Red Admirals, forsaking the buddleia. Not all butterflies enjoy the aesthetically pleasing action of sipping nectar in a pretty flower. The Purple Emperor, perhaps our most impressive butterfly, has a taste for dog dirt and other noisome materials. Often it is the only situation where one can get a photograph of this magnificent insect, as I know from experience.

Quite a number of dead birds, mostly female Chaffinches, have been found locally. Their deaths are caused by a single-cell parasite, *Trichomonas gallinae,* which proliferates in the throats of birds. The disease can be helped to spread by a lack of hygiene around bird-tables. It has been suggested that a temporary cessation of feeding might break the cycle. Cleaning the bird-tables and feeders, and moving them to a fresh area in the garden, would also help. Birds, like people, do not like eating off at a filthy table.

The hot weather has produced the annual nuptial flight of the colony of black ants that live below a flagstone just outside the conservatory. The hot weather may also have had an effect on the local moth population. Two species have been caught two months after their normal flight time, perhaps signifying that they have produced another generation, as happens in the south of England.

We have passed the equinox. The weather, though warm, is windy and there has been some very welcome rain. We have been blessed with a rich harvest of brambles and the elders are bowed under umbrellas of glossy black berries.

October

Summer seems to be carrying on. Though the calendar tells us it is autumn the weather is anything but autumnal, with buttercups and dandelions in full flower. Some of the garden plants have been producing a second flowering and the butterflies, particularly the Red Admirals, refuse to disappear. A favourite source of nectar for these insects has been the ivy flowers, of which I have never known such abundance. Six Comma butterflies have been seen feeding together on Michaelmas daisies. A Large White butterfly caterpillar was feeding on the nasturtiums in the latter half of October. I continue to catch several species of moth much later in the year than their normal flight time, again suggesting that another generation has been produced. I must be about the only gardener locally who has not had a visit from a Hummingbird Hawkmoth. This fascinating day-flying migrant from Southern Europe and North Africa resembles a tiny hummingbird. It hovers in front of a flower whilst feeding, just as its avian namesake does. It has never been as abundant as it is this year.

One denizen of the garden noticeable by its absence is the Hedgehog. I have not seen one of these prickly urchins in the garden during the last few years. Neither have I seen any flattened remains on the nearby roads. The reason for this may be that they have evolved the strategy to run, and not curl up, at the approach of a vehicle. A recent study suggests that the near-extinction of Hedgehogs in the countryside may be associated with the increase in badger numbers. 'Hedgehogs have been eliminated where badger densities are highest', quotes a well-known natural history magazine. My garden is hardly overrun with badgers!

During the recent very mild weather a Woodpigeon has taken to lying flat out in the birdbath, enjoying the soothing sensation of cool water on its belly. Smaller birds denied access have carried out their ablutions in the pond, balancing precariously on the edge of the lily pads.

The ponds are ready for their end of season clean out. There is a solid mass of New Zealand pigmyweed, one of the so-called plant invaders. I appreciate that in large bodies of water it is difficult to control, but in a garden pond it can easily be removed by simply pulling out handfuls. This procedure is beneficial in that it reduces the chemical content of the water and as a result there is less chance of an algal bloom. The densely growing weed also gives cover as well as a breeding substrate for many pond creatures. It may even act as a refuge for the fish from marauding Herons.

I once tried to develop a wild flower meadow but found the maintenance of it difficult in a modest garden. I have seen several flower-meadows in other gardens in the neighbourhood. They are probably successful because they cover a much larger area than I could provide. Another issue is that of growing nettles as a food-source for the larvae of Vanessid butterflies such as Peacocks and Small Tortoiseshells. Only once have I had a butterfly, a Peacock, laying eggs on a nettle patch in the garden, there being plenty of other nettle patches in the area for them to choose. As a result I do not now cultivate nettles in the garden. I was pleased to hear my views and actions vindicated in a recent radio broadcast about wildlife gardening. It was even suggested that it was acceptable to grow some non-native plants and shrubs in the wildlife garden!

November
We are moving into November and the garden is sodden, the lawn is waterlogged. It is hard to remember that only a few months ago we were in the grip of a near-drought. Lately I have been cutting down bushes and lowering the height of some trees by up to ten feet. This growth was along the south and southwest sides of the
garden. Light is so important for healthy growth and because of the increasing shade the water-lilies had not flowered well, even during our tropical July. I have cut up the branches with a chainsaw. The logs I stacked on a log-pile and piled up the brash behind. Both habitats hopefully will become the home for minibeasts and small mammals.

All through the summer the soft garden weeds and household vegetable scraps have been placed in compost bins. They never seem to get any fuller as the contents settle between additions. This material eventually will make good compost for the garden. A tedious task at this time of the year is the collection of leaves. These have been raked up and placed in perforated black bin-bags where they will decompose over the next eighteen months and produce leaf mould for mulching and mixing with the compost.

Another seasonal chore that I very much dislike is the removal of leaves from the ponds. It is one of the laws of cussedness that leaves will be blown into a pond but cannot be blown out. During windy weather the ponds collect more than their fair share of windblown leaves. In previous years I have covered the ponds with netting to catch the falling leaves. This can be a nuisance as it interferes with some of the pond plants and may impede the movement of frogs into the pond where they will hibernate. This year I have chosen to remove the leaves by hand, a rather painful process in very cold weather. If the water vegetation is not thinned out until the spring, it will stop the leaves sinking to the bottom and they are then much more easily removed.

December

I have been pleased to see again a dainty grey, black and yellow bird with a bobbing long tail around the garden ponds, picking off flies from the water's edge. It also lightly hops from one lily-pad to another to retrieve a drowned moth or beetle. This, the Grey Wagtail, is a welcome sight in the winter wildlife garden.

This year, perhaps due to the mild weather, there has not been much of an influx of Long-tailed Field-mice into the basement and garage. One individual did decide to make my birdseed store its retreat, its presence being advertised by the usual signs of droppings and seed shell fragments. These garden-dwelling cousins of the House Mouse are also known as Wood Mice, and are identified by the yellow-brown fur of their upper parts. They are perhaps Britain's commonest mammal and have the unenviable distinction of being a considerable part of the staple diet of many predatory birds and mammals.

A few days ago I glanced out of my window to see a tiny pink, black and white ball with a long black and white tail flitting through the branches in the apple tree. It was followed by another and then another. They progressed in a loose file taking short flights, all moving purposefully in the same direction. They were a party of a dozen Long-tailed Tits working their way through the branches searching for tiny insects and spiders, communicating with each other in quiet lisping calls. They have not been visiting the bird-table and feeders recently, as the mild weather has provided them with sufficient natural food.

To increase the number and variety of moths, specific shrubs and plants can be grown in the garden, leaves of which are the food source for caterpillars or larvae. Each one of the plants listed below is the food plant of at least five different moth species. They are buddleia, shrubby potentilla, cherry-plum, roses, spotted deadnettle, willows, redcurrant, hawthorn, marguerite, sweet marjoram, Michaelmas daisy, perennial candytuft, nettle and parsley. Be pleased if you find these plants covered with caterpillars, for as well as turning into interesting and attractive insects, they are also food for many species of bird.

2007

Snowdrops

January

On New Year's Eve we were about to set off down the drive, only to find that we were trapped by a fallen tree. In the branches was a large Woodpigeons' nest that had been reused many times over the years. Fortunately there were no eggs or young in the nest. The wind was horrendous and several other trees were damaged. After I had cut a way through with a chainsaw, I contacted a local tree surgeon to remove the debris and to cut down two other trees that had begun to look unsafe. He could not come for some days as, unsurprisingly, he had had many other emergency call-outs. This delay was fortuitous as when he did arrive it was again blowing a gale and another tree had blown down. The garden was waterlogged and standing water lay on the lawns. I have never known the weather to be so mild in January. Buttercups and dandelions are showing splashes of yellow and the grass is growing. On the fourth of January snowdrops were showing flashes of white among their green shoots. The plants are confused by the unseasonable warmth, and so are the birds. Blue and Great Tits are voicing their repetitive songs and on 8th January a Song Thrush fluted a few notes. On the same day two cock Blackbirds exhibited territorial behaviour, chasing each other around the garden, as if it were spring.

With several nest-boxes blown down or damaged I have decided to renumber them and give a short description to each one, for example 'closed-fronted on birch near drive'. This will help with recording in the spring. There are over thirty boxes and only about eight will be occupied, but it will give the birds a choice. I have placed two terraced sparrow-boxes, one on the house wall and one in the hedge. I hope that either House or Tree Sparrows will occupy them. The latter birds for many years have been quite scarce, but recently have been increasing in numbers locally. As yet I have not seen any in the garden. They can be distinguished from the slightly more robust House Sparrows by their brown-coloured crowns and black cheek-spots. The males and females are nearly identical, unlike House Sparrows.

The RSPB Garden Bird Watch took place on the last weekend in January. In my garden the result was very disappointing! One had to record, in the space of one hour, each species of bird seen within the confines of one's garden, and the maximum number seen at any one time. My meagre count consisted of one each of Chaffinch, Blackbird, Collared Dove, Woodpigeon and Carrion Crow. There were two each of Blue, Great and Coal Tits, also two Robins and three House Sparrows. I was not alone in observing few birds. It was interesting to note on the Garden Bird Survey website that many other recorders expressed their disappointment at the small numbers of birds seen.

I feel the results are very dependent on the weather conditions. At the time of my survey, 11 a.m. to 12 noon on 28th January, there was a very strong cool wind and most of the birds I did manage to see were sheltering. How many birds were present in my garden at that time but hidden I do not know. I consider that the weather conditions should be taken into account, especially if these conditions are widespread throughout the country. A more accurate set of results would be to take the average of observations over several days. If I had carried out the survey the following day I would have recorded much higher numbers, and more species. The weather was calm and warmer, encouraging many of the resident garden birds to come out of their sheltered positions.

February

At the beginning of February I saw a Song Thrush feeding in the garden. This was the first sighting for several months, though I have heard one singing from 29th January onwards. Every year the thrushes disappear in late autumn only to reappear in late winter and early spring. Another welcome visitor to the garden was a Spring Usher moth, found in my moth-trap on the morning of the same day. This insect, as its name describes, appears in early spring, though earlier in a mild season. It is the first moth I have caught this year. The absence of moths is likely to be due to the extremely windy weather. The female of the Spring Usher, along with other winter-emerging moths, is flightless.

Several birds are starting to show signs of the approaching nesting season. A pair of Great Tits spent some time inspecting a nest-box and a pair of Collared Doves collected fine twigs for nest construction. A few days ago, on looking out of the window, I saw a brown and white mouse-like bird spiralling up a tree trunk, probing with its fine curved bill. This behaviour is typical of a Treecreeper, which of course it was. It then flew to the ground and began probing the soil and moss-covered stones with its bill, behaviour that I think is untypical.

I have never known ivy to bear so much fruit as this year. In late autumn it was covered in flowers and, as a result, with nectaring moths. Now the fruits provide easy pickings for a pair of Woodpigeons, busy nest prospecting in the ivy-covered apple tree. It has become firmly rooted since it was blown over in 2005 and stayed locked in place during the recent gales. It originally fell against neighbouring apple trees, which prop it up. It has become a feature in the garden, an arbour under which I have placed some flagstones and a table and chairs. It will be a pleasant place to sit out in the summer.

A few days ago I heard the loud challenging song of a Mistle Thrush emanating from an elevated position during a period of high wind, as if to justify its alternative name of Storm-cock. More recently on 6th February I heard the cheery cascading song of a Chaffinch. However during the recent spell of what now counts as wintry weather in these snowless times, their songs have temporarily been silenced. I am now waiting for the first fluting notes of a Blackbird. It usually begins singing later than its thrush cousins, a true harbinger of spring.

March

I had an interesting letter in response to my observations of a ground-feeding Treecreeper. The writer, a naturalist who lives some ten miles to the east of me, had observed the same phenomenon. He had also seen one picking up the fine crumbs under a feeder, and even clinging on it for a few seconds.

A cock Pheasant has been visiting the garden over the last few days, haughtily striding about picking up spilt grain under the bird-table. He, if it is the same one, appears each spring, perhaps seeking out a female. A different bird, a female, hurled itself into a bush the other day. A beautiful hen Sparrowhawk dashed after a small bird, which, thankfully for the bird, it missed. It sat for a few minutes while it switched off its autopilot before flapping its wings and gliding over the hedge. The frequent visits of this fierce little raptor to the garden are indicative of a large resident population of small birds, essential if the hawk is to survive. I welcome their presence.

I have been watching the courtship of a pair of Woodpigeons. The male follows the female on the lawn, bowing and raising its tail. Recently another pair has begun to frequent the garden and there have been some fights. It will be interesting to see if they start nesting. The longer-term residents have already built their nest in a cupressus tree. A hen Blackbird started to build its nest on 10th March, using debris I had removed from one of the ponds when carrying out a spring clean.

The garden is now a hive of activity for nesting birds. On 13th March a pair of Starlings adopted the nest-box outside the study window, one of the two adapted from redundant music-centre speakers. A pair of Great Tits was also inspecting it, but the entrance hole was too large for their liking. On the same day a Blackbird completed its nest in the cupressus hedge. For several days I have been watching two pairs of Greenfinches trying to claim an ivy-festooned apple tree as their nesting site. On 21st March I watched a male Greenfinch carrying building material into the dense ivy and at the same time I saw a hen Greenfinch carrying material into the hedge where the Blackbird had built its nest. The two pairs of Greenfinches are therefore building, having sorted out their respective claims to building sites. Both sexes take part in the nest construction. Interestingly the female was collecting feathers for the nest, though the literature does not appear to record that feathers are used as a nest lining.

April

Two pairs of Robins are building in the garden, one in ivy on the house wall and the other in ivy on the bole of a hawthorn tree. The latter bird is extremely confiding, picking up dead leaves at my feet and flying backwards and forwards to its nest. While this activity was taking place a pair of Carrion Crows landed on trees in the garden and started to inspect the area. Crows will rob the nests of other birds and I thought they were perhaps looking for eggs that had been laid early, but instead they began to twist off small hazel twigs. It would have been much easier for them to pick up fallen twigs from the ground. I suppose that they prefer living material, as it is more pliable and so easier to weave into the nest bowl.

A few days ago the goldfish could not be seen and the water was turgid. It was obvious that the Heron had paid a return visit. I had not strung twine over this pond. The fish in the protected pond were still all present and the water was clear. The twine had deterred the Heron. I have since caught a fleeting glimpse of a goldfish in the disturbed pond. There may still be some others in hiding. I have previously found that if a Heron visits a pond, the fish that survive can remain hidden for weeks afterwards.

Once again not a single frog has been seen this spring. Perhaps the Heron has taken the frogs too, or alternatively they have died out through inbreeding. They originated from spawn collected over twenty years ago and there are no other frog colonies nearby. I have collected frog-spawn from a different source and placed it in the ponds. There may be breeding frogs in the ponds again within a few years.

Towards the end of March the weather quickly warmed up and on 27th there were several sightings of Peacock butterfly in the garden. The warm weather had brought them out of hibernation. On the same day two Small

White butterflies were seen. They spend the winter as pupae, and their emergence as adults is very early. They have probably emerged early because of the unseasonably warm weather. Let's hope they are harbingers of a warm and sunny spring to come.

May

The Robin that has built in the ivy on the house wall is sitting on five eggs. I hope they do not suffer the same fate as that of a Song Thrush that also built in ivy. In early April it was sitting on four beautiful blue eggs. Some days later I found a blue egg lying intact on the ground. On inspecting the thrushes' nest I found, sadly, that it was empty. Carrion Crows and Jackdaws visit the garden, and one of them could have been the robber, but why should one egg be left and unbroken? Another one of the many riddles presented in the machinations of the wildlife garden.

A different visitor could have been the culprit. For several days I have been hearing a coughing chuckle, hyena-like, and sometimes catching a glimpse of the long-tailed black-and-white bird responsible for that noise. I have an ambivalent attitude to the presence of Magpies in the garden. I find them interesting and attractive but they have a deleterious effect on nesting songbirds. They have nested in the garden before but they themselves have become victims of nearby nesting Carrion Crows. Another corvid that has become a garden resident is a Jackdaw with a damaged wing. While its nesting contemporaries have been collecting twigs to block the neighbourhood chimneys it has been hopping about the garden making short clumsy flights. It pays frequent visits to the bird-table, apparently its main source of food.

During the recent very warm spell many butterflies have visited the garden. These include Peacocks and Small Tortoiseshells, which hibernate as adults. An interesting early visitor has been a Comma butterfly. Over the last decade it has become resident in our area.

The Starlings are sitting on full clutches of eggs. One box is only a foot away from clothes drying on a washing line. This does not seem to bother the birds. However a bird that *was* in bother was a cock Chaffinch. It flew straight into the conservatory window and knocked itself out. I brought the bird in and kept it warm. After an hour it had recovered enough to be placed outside, and it then flew away. If left outside it might

172

have become a victim of a crow or cat before it could recover.

June

The weather changed about the middle of May to what we normally expect at this time of year. The unseasonably warm sunny weather we experienced after Easter changed to much fresher, windier and wetter weather. The rain however came at just the right time after the warm dry spell and the garden plants are growing rapidly. The May blossom burst into all its glory at the end of April and other wild flowers are all flowering early. When we arrived home from a fortnight's holiday, the Robins, Blackbirds and a brood of Starlings had fledged. In the nest-box on the tree to which the clothesline was fastened were young starlings about a week old. The parents fed their young even when the washing was being pegged out only two metres away. The raucous screech of the parents and young filled the garden. Two days ago four of the five young left. The fifth youngster had refused to leave the box and the exasperated parents, which were feeding its four siblings in the surrounding branches, refused to feed it until it joined the rest. It finally left home two days later.

I had placed two terraced nest-boxes in the garden hoping to entice either House or Tree Sparrows, but with no luck. However, in one compartment of a terrace is a somewhat late-nesting Great Tit sitting on six eggs. For the first time in over twenty years not one pair of Blue Tits has used any of the nest-boxes in the garden. On the plus side three pairs of Robins, and possibly a fourth, are currently nesting.

A Song Thrush has built its nest in the spindly twigs of a forsythia bush. A previous nest that it had built was robbed. I thought the new nest would be blown away from its precarious position during the recent gale-force winds, but it survived and now contains four beautiful sky blue eggs. The droopy-winged Jackdaw, which has stayed around the house for the last month, continues to flop around the garden and seems quite dependent on what I put out on the bird-table. It has to put up with an early morning onslaught from a posse of Rooks. These noisy invaders are not tolerated by the local Woodpigeons, however, which attempt to drive them away.

The other day a carcass of a nearly fledged Woodpigeon lay on the drive. Most of the flesh had been stripped from its breast. It had all the hallmarks of a Sparrowhawk kill. I am always amazed at how much of its victim a Sparrowhawk can eat! A Woodpigeon is considerably heavier than its killer. Usually these fierce little hawks feed almost exclusively on small birds. If they are unwelcome visitors to your garden there are several ways to discourage them. Half-filled plastic bottles or old CDs hung up in the trees should scare them away. If your feeders are under tree-branches, you can hang strings like bead curtain strands a few inches apart round the area to slow down the hawks. One can even stick bamboo canes on the lawn to slow down a fast approach. Personally I would prefer to have a visit from one of these fierce little fliers rather than have all this paraphernalia in the garden.

July

This year there has been an absence of Blue Tits using the nest-boxes in the garden. A local naturalist who is responsible for the management of many nest-boxes has told me that in fact this year more Great Tits than Blue Tits have used the boxes. Normally Blue Tits outnumber Great Tits in a ratio of two to one. Incidentally, I eventually removed the eggs of the Great Tit which had been sitting on six eggs. They were obviously infertile, as she had been sitting for more than twice the normal incubation period of two weeks. This is not an action that I normally carry out but I felt sorry for her sitting pointlessly and there may have been a chance of her laying again.

Sadly I found the body of a dead Jackdaw. It is probably the one with the drooping wing that had been flopping around the garden for several weeks and was dependent on the offerings on the bird-table.

Another disappointment was the taking of the four Song Thrush's eggs from a nest built in an insecure position in the spindly twigs of the forsythia bush. This is the second time the thrushes have been robbed. The culprit may have been the local Magpie. It visits the garden regularly scouring the bushes for eggs and young birds. It always sounds as if it is laughing. I hope this attractive but efficient predator will not find the Greenfinch, which laid five eggs and now has three young in a nest near the end of the clothesline.

This is the third year that there has been no sign of Hedgehogs in the garden. Neither have my neighbours' gardens been visited by these prickly friends of gardeners. A mile away from me lives a keen gardener who has become the proud owner of a young Hedgehog given by a wildlife refuge. Her extensive wildlife garden should in all rights have had several of these useful insectivores as residents.

Moths caught in the moth-trap have increased in number and diversity during this period of warm weather. Several species are new to the garden this year, including a Small Elephant Hawkmoth, a moth much less common than its larger namesake, the Elephant Hawkmoth. As I empty the trap I have to be wary of the waiting gang of birds hoping to have a free lunch out of the moth catch.

August *(1)*

I have never before known almost tropical weather conditions with localised storms such as we have experienced this summer. But at least there are plenty of worms in the moist ground for the Blackbirds and Robins. As well as the abundance of worms, many birds have been feeding on the heavy crop of fruit on the cherry tree. For some days a pair of Blackbirds has been feeding on the berries, chasing away any others of their kind and keeping the harvest for themselves. They in turn were chased away by Jackdaws, which also began to feed on the cherries. I have never before seen Jackdaws feeding in this way. The ground is littered with cherrystones.

On looking out of the window some days ago, my attention was drawn to what appeared to be a large brown bumblebee buzzing across my field of vision, then another and another. They were in fact a brood of fledgling Wrens leaving a nest just below the window. I had completely overlooked this nest. It was not far from a cock nest that I had previously found, but which was not chosen by the hen to lay her eggs. The baby Wrens were completely spherical, the tiny uplifted tail of the adult not yet developed. Their parents appeared on the scene, each carrying a small earthworm in its bill.

Some weeks ago my attention had been drawn by the continuous *'ze ze'* call of a Greenfinch, an indication that there must be a nest in the immediate vicinity. Sure enough, a nest containing five eggs was found just above the basement door, close to where the clothesline was attached to the wall. In spite of disturbance caused by the opening and closing of the door and the movement of the clothesline, four young Greenfinches successfully fledged. I have found that even if there is some disturbance to a nesting bird, as long as one is careful and does not make sudden movements and sounds, the sitting bird can become accustomed to one's presence and will not desert.

There have been some hot spells resulting in butterflies visiting the garden. Red Admirals, Small Tortoiseshells, Peacocks and Painted Ladies have visited the nectar-laden flowers of the buddleia. Recently a Comma butterfly spent some time sunning itself on the climbing rose. As is now well known, these ragged orange-coloured butterflies have moved north into our area during the last decade, though they have not noticeably increased in number. Commas have two generations a year and it is now the time of year when the caterpillars of the second generation might be found feeding, usually on nettles. Initially they feed on the underside of the leaf but when nearly fully-grown the caterpillars feed on the upper surface. The white coloration on their backs gives the impression to any prospective predator that they are bird-droppings and therefore they are left alone.

August *(2)*

Early in August the garden was visited by a dragon. It sailed round the wildlife pond hawking for insects. Its behaviour epitomises its name, a hawker dragonfly. In fact it was a female Southern Hawker. As its name also signifies it originally was a southern species, though it is moving north and for the last decade or two has become quite common in our area. The beautiful lime-green bands on its thorax distinguish it from the similar Common Hawker. I was hoping it would lay eggs in the wildlife pond but I did not observe it doing so. After some hours it flew away. The young, or nymphs, of this dragonfly are voracious predators and would find the numerous young newts in the ponds delicious eating. The ponds are teeming with newt larvae so I would not miss a few. Recently, while collecting some of these young amphibians to give to a fellow naturalist, I found two young newts much bigger and stockier than their fellows. These were young Great Crested Newts. I was very pleased that this protected species had bred again this year, along with both Common and Palmate Newts.

The weather has been somewhat inclement, but we have enjoyed some warm days and on one of these I watched a female Blackbird sunning itself. It was oblivious to its surroundings, its beak wide open. Nearby was a

Comma butterfly sunning itself on a green plastic garden chair to which it returned time and time again, after replenishing itself from the honey-rich buddleia. It would be nice to know that they were regularly breeding here and were not just visitors. As if in answer to that question, a friend recently let me know that he had witnessed, in his garden in Kirkoswald, the emergence from its chrysalis of a Comma butterfly. The caterpillar appeared to have been feeding on gooseberry leaves. There is some variation in the life cycle of this butterfly. Some caterpillars of the first brood develop slowly and do not mature in time to produce a second generation. Thus there can be both caterpillars and butterflies at the same time.

Nasturtiums are grown in the garden, not only for their somewhat garish colours, but also to provide food for the white butterflies. There are often clusters of large yellow caterpillars, the larvae of the Large White butterfly, found on the upper surface of nasturtium leaves. Some weeks ago however I watched a female Small White butterfly pressing the tip of her abdomen to the surface of the nasturtium leaves. She laid the eggs singly, and usually only one on each leaf, on either the upper surface or the underside of the leaf. I shall look forward to the development of her green caterpillars. The close relative of the white butterflies, the Orange-tip butterfly, lays its eggs singly on crucifers, such as jack-by-the-hedge (garlic mustard). The caterpillars are cannibals, so if another female comes along and lays another egg there will be dire consequences for the younger and therefore smaller caterpillar when it hatches.

September

After a visit in August of a dragon (fly), this month two heavily made-up ladies graced the garden, Painted Lady butterflies They were both in pristine condition with a pink flush to their wings, looking as if they had very recently emerged from their chrysalises. These large colourful insects cannot survive our damp cool winters, though early migrants to our shores can breed here, and may have several broods. They usually lay their eggs on thistles, though other plants, including nettles, may be used. Accompanying these ladies were several beautiful Red Admirals. These are also immigrants and until recently it was thought that they too could not survive our winters, but there have been reports of them being seen in December and January, perhaps as a result of our increasingly mild winters.

There has been an influx of both Large and Small White butterflies, attracted to the nasturtiums on which both species have been laying eggs. The eggs of the Small White have hatched, but the conspicuous orange eggs, laid in batches, of the Large White have disappeared. They must have become the victim of some mini predator.

As I was sitting in the garden with a butterfly book, reminding myself of the difference in wing patterns of the different white butterflies, a visitor darted in and sat on the book as if to acquaint itself with such definitive differences. It darted off, and then came back to sit on my hand. As its behaviour implied, it was a darter, a female Common Darter. It could have mistaken the bright sunlight shining on the book for a patch of water. This small dragonfly is found in large numbers in its usual watery environment. The garden does not offer it a suitable habitat.

Large numbers of a species of wasp have been flying round the trees in the garden. They are somewhat smaller than the common social wasps, of which there have been very few this year. For the third year running they have made their home in the eves of the house. These wasps are not a nuisance, as their flight path is well above head height and they are beneficial in reducing the number of flies. Interestingly, large numbers of these small insects are also found in the moth-trap when I empty it every morning. As the light on the trap does not come on until after sunset, they must have been flying in the dark. The last time I used the trap there were over a hundred individuals.

Swallows are assembling on the telephone wires and Robins have started to sing again. The hedges are covered with hips, haws and elderberries, and the brambles are heavy with blackberries. Sadly nothing lasts, as the plaintive winter song of the Robin seems to say.

October

On 22nd September my attention was drawn to the sight of a brownish middle-sized butterfly flitting among the flowers in the garden. When it settled I could see that its wings were chocolate-brown in colour, with a pattern of creamy-yellow patches, a Speckled Wood. This normally woodland-dwelling butterfly is common in the south and the midlands, as well as areas of the north and west Highlands of Scotland. Until very recently it was only found in the extreme south of Cumbria. However during the last month I had heard reports that singletons had been seen near Penrith and also in High Stand Plantation, four miles to the south of my garden. I was ready to search for it in High Stand, but one of its kind had come to visit me in the garden. On seeing it, I rushed for my camera to photograph it before it flew away. Happily it stayed for the rest of that day and was seen for some hours the following day. The food plants for its caterpillars are no problem as they feed on various species of common grasses so I hope this butterfly is here to stay.

On returning from a week's holiday, we found clumps of spherical currant-sized objects arranged in a curve some metres across on the lawn. Their size and shape identified them as rabbit-droppings. It is said that rabbits often produce these latrines to mark the boundaries of their territory. Strangely enough we have not caught even a glimpse of these potential pests in the garden for several years. We did find one small mammal in the garden, a dead shrew lying on a step. Whether the animal that had killed it found it to be unpalatable I do not know, but frequently complete corpses of these small insectivores are found left in some exposed place in the garden. From its size I assumed it was a Common Shrew and not a Pigmy Shrew, which also lives in the garden.

The weather has remained extremely mild, and now, in the middle of October many spring and summer flowers, such as dandelions and buttercups, are blooming again. There is a rich crop of fungi. One of the few species I can identify is the Shaggy Inkcap or 'Lawyers' Wig'. Their caps emerged like magic, pristine creamy-white and buff, from the ground, but within a day they became discoloured, then finally black and producing black inky fluid. It is said that this fungus is edible while the gills are still white. However I will give it a miss, as I do all fungi, unless they are bought in a shop.

The moths now being caught in the trap are all indicators of autumn with names like Autumnal Moth and November Moth. They belong to a small group which are extremely difficult to separate for identification. Fortunately a recent arrival in our area is easy to recognise. It is the Blair's Shoulder-Knot, several specimens of which I have already caught this autumn. This moth was first recorded in Britain in 1951 on the Isle of Wight. Over the years it has moved north and I recorded it in my garden in 1999. Is this another example, along with the arrival of the Speckled Wood butterfly in our area, of the result of climate change? The young leaves of Leyland cypress are amongst its food plants so there should be no shortage of these moths in British gardens.

November

This dark time of year is not all doom and gloom. Recently our spirits were uplifted by the chuckling calls of Fieldfares from Scandinavia. These large grey thrushes passed low overhead in considerable flocks on 23rd October. A day or two later their smaller cousins, the Redwings, followed, though not in such large numbers, and also not so vocal. Also passing over the garden at dusk, in a huge conglomeration of V-shaped skeins, were many hundreds of geese returning to the Solway from their feeding-grounds in the Eden valley.

In the garden itself there has also been activity. Four Rooks gathered in the hedge. Two of them were tearing twigs off the branches of an ash tree. Whether this was early courtship or even very early nest building I could not decide. The weather has again been unseasonably mild this autumn. Roses are in full bloom and some spring garden plants are flowering. Red Admiral butterflies were flying well into November and on the seventh of the month a bumblebee was nectaring on borage, self-seeded in the rockery.

Some days ago, when cutting back the shrubs, I was reminded of a horror film. Quietly and relentlessly a hop plant had completely smothered a large lilac tree. This climber was in the garden when I moved in over twenty years ago. Each year it grew rapidly, never getting out of hand and dying back each winter. However this year it has raced away. Its climbing stems are very difficult to dislodge and are extremely tough. It also seems to sprout from many different places on the ground. Truly a horror of a vegetable. I shall be ready for it next spring with spade and shears.

The last day of October was a good drying day and after the washing was brought in from the garden to be ironed, we were amazed to find a butterfly on a pair of trousers. It was a Comma, perched with its wings closed, showing the light comma mark on the dark underside of its wings. It may have crawled into one of the trouser legs thinking it was a good

Fieldfares

place to spend the winter and got a rude awakening when brought into the house. I carefully carried it into the garden shed and placed it in a corner behind the shelf. I hope it will survive the winter. If it is a female it may lay eggs in the spring and start a colony in the garden, something to look forward to.

December
Up to the beginning of December little rain had fallen but in the first nine days of December there were two inches of rain. I have recently bought a simple rain gauge, which I check and empty each morning. I was aware that we have had little rain this autumn and as a result some of the recently planted shrubs were somewhat distressed. Unlike most people I have

wanted the weatherman to promise rain. Now, with this modest two inches, the garden is looking well watered and the shrubs have perked up. At this time of year everything remains sodden. Because the temperature is low and the humidity high there is little evaporation. Rain falls frequently but rarely heavily in England. We tend to think that we have had much more rain than we actually have had. Except for an odd night of frost the autumn has been mild.

Nearly all the deciduous trees have lost their leaves and birds' nests, hidden during the summer, have been revealed. A foot away from the basement door I found the tiny twiggy nest of a Dunnock and hidden in the brush on a tree trunk, which I passed close by regularly, were the mossy remains of a Chaffinch nest. During the spring I had heard the excited *'pink'*-ing call of the parent birds when I walked by, so I knew a nest was in the vicinity but had not realised it was so close. It is well worthwhile walking round the garden looking for used birds nests and seeing if one can identify their owners.

Some days ago I was sorry to pick up the corpse of a delicate brown and light grey bird with a long fine curved bill. It was a Treecreeper, the tiny bird one can see spiralling up a tree trunk as it searches for insects under the bark. It had quite obviously flown into a window and killed itself. All the main windows have silhouettes of hawks to scare off small birds and up till now there have not been any casualties under these windows. I must buy some more silhouettes for the smaller windows.

Another tragedy was finding the corpse of a field-mouse in an empty container which had been used for storing bird food. The smell had drawn me to the sad sight. The mouse had managed to squeeze in but could not possibly grip the smooth sides to force its way out. It had starved to death, for which I was very sorry and I will double my efforts to see that small animals cannot enter any container. Many small mammals die in bottles thrown out of car windows into hedgerows. They crawl in and cannot get out.

The Treecreeper could have been looking for a Winter Moth. I caught a male in the moth-trap, a drab little insect. The female moth is flightless, so that she and her valuable cargo of eggs cannot be blown away in the winter gales. I recently caught five specimens of another species of moth that flies at this time of year. These insects, appropriately called December

Moths, are much more attractive. Four of these moths were males, small with feathery antennae. The larger and fatter one was a female, which I kept for a short time to photograph. On removing her from the container I found she had laid about fifty eggs. I am keeping these until they hatch out in the spring.

Great Spotted Woodpecker

January

Spring appeared to start on the morning of 30th December. Birdsong was heard, particularly the strident *'teacher-teacher'* of a Great Tit, and the first snowdrops were coming into flower. This mild weather followed a protracted cold spell in the latter half of December which had encased the garden ponds with a covering of ice over two inches thick. I found the corpses of three golden orfe lying under the ice, which I tried to break into without success. I did not hit too hard as the shockwaves could have stunned the remaining fish. I assumed that the layer of ice had stopped gaseous exchange taking place and that there had been a build-up of carbon dioxide in the pond. It may be that orfe are less resistant to these conditions than goldfish, which have remained perfectly healthy. I should have tried to keep an area of water ice-free by floating a tennis ball or cracking the ice before it got too thick!

I was given a nestbox camera system as a Christmas present. This consists of a closed nest box incorporating a miniature video camera. It can be connected to a TV, and hopefully one can have a close-up view of nesting birds. I have sited it in a sheltered position facing north, just outside the conservatory window. The problem is, how do I encourage tits to choose that particular box in which to nest? I have similar boxes placed around the garden, which could be chosen in preference to the camera nest-box. I could remove all other boxes in the vicinity but that could jeopardise the chances of birds nesting at all. I cannot think how to persuade any tit with aspirations to be a TV star, to appear on this 'candid camera'.

I sometimes visit a garden in Penton where regular feeding has attracted large flocks of birds. Of particular interest is a flock of Goldfinches, which hover around the feeders like a swarm of golden butterflies. The main attraction for them is a nyjer – or niger – seed-dispenser. They find these tiny black seeds irresistible. I was given such a seed-feeder and have hung it on the bird-table. As yet no Goldfinch has found it. I would be delighted if it attracted a permanent flock of these gorgeous little finches.

From the end of the year, particularly at dusk, I heard the strident alarm notes of Blackbirds. I assumed they were not happy at the presence of a young Tawny Owl that had been chased out of its parents' territory in a nearby wood and was roosting in the high cupressus hedge. It upsets the resident garden birds when it becomes active at dusk. However, it turned out that the calls were emitted by two sparring cock Blackbirds. For several days, often at first light and also at dusk they fling themselves up into the air and start fighting. They are obviously determining the boundaries of their future nesting territories, so early before the breeding season! One male had his brown mate in tow and she sneakily slipped in to give his opponent a peck. The other cock bird did not appear to have a mate. I wonder if the males establish territories in the middle of winter before they gain a mate or do they pair up first? It will be interesting to see where the two nests will be built. Will they be equidistant from the dividing line along which they fight?

February

As I have done for the last few years I carried out the RSPB garden bird count on 27th January. One is required to record the maximum number of each species seen at one time during one hour of watching. I recorded ten bird species, including four House Sparrows and three each of Collared Doves and Woodpigeons. One must resist the temptation to add birds seen just before and after the hour. I heard three Robins singing at the same time though I only actually saw one. I had resisted the urge to scatter loaves of bread, fat and seeds over the garden in order to increase the number of birds for my count. This would have been comparable to the actions of an angler who uses ground bait to attract fish to his patch. The number of species I counted in the specified hour was less than when not carrying out a count. I even had a mischievous suspicion that neighbours were trying to attract my birds to their gardens with tasty bribes, causing a depletion of my numbers. This was, of course, in my imagination.

During the count I was intrigued by the antics of a pair of Woodpigeons. They kept flying up from the ground trying to land on each other's back. After some time one of the duellists raised one wing as if it was a gesture of submission before waddling away. I do not know if it was a mating display or rivalry between two males.

Some days ago, during one of the very mild spells we have had this winter, I decided to clean out the two ornamental ponds. In the process, while catching the fish, I removed several newts and placed them in the wildlife pond. The smallest of the ponds is rigid and on lifting it I found that several newts were secreted under the bottom of the pond half a metre down. It is not just toads that are found in holes. The fish were in full view of any passing Heron in the newly cleaned ponds and quickly we crisscrossed tough fishing-line over the ponds to act as a deterrent to these attractive but unwelcome visitors to the garden.

March

From the beginning of February, six Magpies have been displaying in the high cupressus hedge. I hope that a pair might nest in the garden. Twenty years ago, a pair of Magpies built their domed twiggy nest about fifteen feet up in a Sitka spruce. The six eggs hatched and the nestlings were growing well until one morning I found a dead parent below the nest at the bottom of the tree. I believe that a pair of Carrion Crows had killed the unfortunate bird. They were nesting in a tree at the edge of the adjoining field and were intolerant of the proximity of a potential threat to their eggs or young. The other parent Magpie was nowhere to be seen and by the time I forced my way into the extremely well protected nest the young had died. I was sorry that this had happened, even though Magpies take their toll of garden birds, both eggs and young. I like to see these handsome pied birds about the garden, and hear their hoarse laughing calls.

On the morning of 9th February I saw the familiar silhouette of a Song Thrush near the top of the cherry tree. I entered the garden to hear the evocative song of this herald of spring. During the darkest period of winter I never see a thrush in the garden, but every year, a few days before Valentine's day, one appears in the same pose, in the same position, on the same tree and begins to sing. It is another of the first steps of the slow journey into spring. Later in the day I heard the first short bursts of a Chaffinch's song and a few days later the full cascade was produced. Other songbirds have begun their spring chorus, including the jangling song of the Dunnock. All the tits are calling and on 12th I watched a pair of Long-tailed Tits foraging for tiny insects among the twigs and buds. As these birds were a pair and not in a flock, and as they remained for some time in the garden, I am hopeful that they will nest not far away. Even though these tiny birds are so light and delicate they nest very early, often before winter has completely ended.

One morning recently I saw a Sparrowhawk sitting on the roof of the bird-table. It perhaps thought that the feeding station was there to provide it with a breakfast of small birds. It stayed there for some minutes giving me time to admire the plumage pattern and colour of this beautiful little raptor. Needless to say no other birds came to the table and after some time it glided smoothly over the hedge. I welcome these hunters and the Magpies in the garden. They are natural pieces of the garden jigsaw.

There continues to be a shortage of moths in the garden, a situation endorsed by other moth-ers in the county. The third moth I had caught this year, a Pale Brindled Beauty, I carefully released into the bottom of the hedge. Foolishly it flew upwards, whereupon a female Chaffinch

Sparrowhawk

caught it. It took the moth to its perch, removed the wings and devoured it with relish, further depleting the garden moth population.

There were two new visitors to the garden a few days ago. One was a sparrow-sized bird boasting a canary-yellow head and neck. Its brownish, sparrow-like mate accompanied it. They were Yellowhammers, a species of bird that one does not see too frequently nowadays, and a first for my garden. They keep returning to feed on the ground below the bird-table, never on it. We all know its song is likened to *a-little-bit-of-bread-and-no-cheese.* It is also called a scribble-lark because of the scribble-like markings on its eggs. I live in hope that I may be able to see its artwork if it nests in the garden.

April
After Easter I could see no change in the garden from a week before. The journey into spring had been halted and one can only hope that no damage has been done by the nightly frosts and, more seriously, the bitterly cold northerly winds. If we are blessed with a few warm days the journey will resume with renewed vigour, as it always does.

A few days ago I saw a male Sparrowhawk sprawling on the weeds in the large pond, flapping its wings. I thought at first it was drowning but then realised it was enjoying a bath, even though it was a bitterly cold day. I watched it for some minutes before deciding to go and get my camera. However by the time I had fitted my zoom lens it had finished its ablutions and flown up onto an ornamental arch. I managed to take a few hurried shots before it flew away.

Once again there has been no frog-spawn in the garden this year. In fact I have not seen a single frog. I have heard from other naturalists in the area that they too have not seen any of these usually common amphibians in their ponds. Whether this is the result of disease or due to inbreeding in an isolated colony remains a mystery.

A Robin has again built its nest of dry leaves deep in the tangle of the ivy covered apple tree. It is sharing the site with a pair of Greenfinches, which also built there last year. I have never known so many of these sturdy little finches. Several pairs are busy searching for nesting sites. Twice recently the garden has been graced by visits from a pair of Goldfinches but they do not appear to wish to linger. I have for the first time seen a Tree Sparrow in the garden, feeding on the ground below the bird-table. I would like to think that these increasingly common birds could become established in the garden.

May

In the interest of hygiene I have moved the bird-table some metres to a new position near to one of the ponds. This allowed me to clean the old site and so to reduce the chance of a build-up of diseases. Near where the table had stood was the entrance hole of a Long-tailed Field-mouse. This dainty little golden-brown rodent scuttled out to nibble at the seeds dislodged by the birds feeding above. After the move it discontinued its visits during the day, as it must have found it too risky to run the greater distance in full view. However its place has been taken by a grey House Mouse, which pops out of its hole under the lining of the close-by pond in order to feed under the table. It is equally endearing to watch. I am happy to have both species of mouse in the garden, as long as they do not come into the house.

The bird-table has become the centre of much activity. The Long-tailed Tits are back after an absence of two weeks. They prefer the fat balls. For some time these were not available on the table as Rooks ripped them from their net bags. When I placed the balls in feeders one remarkably agile Rook broke into them. It even managed to prise the lid off a heavy feeder while hanging upside down from the table. I have finally managed to display the fat balls in such a way that even this ingenious and acrobatic corvid was beaten. The effort was worthwhile to get the Long-tailed Tits back.

At last I have seen a Goldfinch feeding on the nyjer seed. Three of these butterfly-like birds visit the bird-table. They show more interest in the shelled sunflower seeds than in the nyjer seeds. A trio of Bullfinches has been visiting the garden to eat the opening buds on the apple trees.

Some days ago there was a resounding thwack on the living room window. I looked out expecting to see a pigeon or dove lying dead on the ground, but a Great Spotted Woodpecker was sitting on the ground, looking slightly stunned. The bird had a rectangle of red on its nape advertising that it was an adult male. I kept an eye on it during the time it was on the ground in case a cat found it, but after ten minutes it flew onto the windowsill. A short while later it flew off in its typical dipping manner, no worse for wear. Any other bird species would have been killed by the impact. But as the bird communicates and feeds by bashing its beak against a tree trunk for long periods its skull has evolved to withstand violent knocks.

I also found a stunned female Blackbird that had obviously flown into a window. I brought it into the conservatory and made it comfortable, facing the open door. It is better not to increase the tension of a stunned bird by mollycoddling it but to leave it alone, giving it the opportunity to fly off when ready. Leaving it outside to recover is tantamount to offering it as a sacrifice to our neighbourhood feline friends or to a passing opportunistic corvid. Fortunately the Blackbird slowly started to revive and after an hour made a successful but somewhat drunken flight into a nearby bush from which it eventually flew away.

June

A Sparrowhawk recently dashed into the garden, scattering the birds at the bird table, and perched on the back of a nearby garden seat. It then dropped onto the ground and scuttled under the adjacent holly bush as if searching for hiding birds. After a minute or so it gave up and flew away. I have seen them dive suicidally into a bush when chasing a fleeing bird, but it is the first time I have witnessed behaviour that seems to indicate premeditation.

Two pairs of Starlings are each rearing four young in the converted music-centre speakers and a Wren is sitting on six eggs in its domed nest of dried leaves outside the bedroom window. The cock had built several cock nests and the hen had chosen this one and lined it with feathers before laying her eggs. A pair of very trusting Blackbirds is feeding young in full view, above the basement door.

The Robin, whose nest had been destroyed, has built again in the same tree only two feet from its previous nest. There was one egg on 16th April and another egg was laid the next day. On 19th April there were still only two eggs in the nest. They were cold and I thought the parents had deserted. I did not look again until April 23rd when to my surprise found four eggs. Early on the morning of 25th April there were five eggs, and the parent began to sit. Was the break in egg laying due to the very cold weather we experienced in April? When we returned from holiday on May 10th there were four young and one egg in the nest so at least one of the 'cold' eggs had survived! Sadly on 12th May I found a dead Robin on the ground only a few feet from the nest, and on inspection found the very young nestlings cold and hardly moving. I was hoping that the other parent would have tried rearing them, in which case we could have left them in the nest and tried to supplement their food. As it was we tried to revive and feed them but they were very small and died in spite of all our efforts. This was particularly sad, as it was a second unsuccessful nesting.

I can now relate a happier event. I had fixed the nest-box with a built-in video camera to the wall just outside the conservatory window, checked that the system was working, and then forgot about it. When we returned from holiday I found that a Blue Tit was sitting on nine eggs in the box. We set up the camera and connected it to the television in the kitchen. We got surprisingly good pictures of the mother brooding. On 18th May the eggs began hatching and by the following morning seven eggs had hatched. A parent bird was observed apparently eating an eggshell from which a baby bird had hatched. On 22nd May there is no sign of the remaining two eggs and the seven young are growing fast. Let's hope that the outcome is different from that of the Robins.

July

There have been a series of disasters in the wildlife garden. The Blue Tit in the box with the video camera laid nine eggs, of which seven hatched.

After several days the number was reduced to three young. Finally after twelve days there appeared to be only one young left in the box. The youngster could hardly open its beak when caterpillars were brought to it. The parent kept pecking it to try to make it open its beak. It was very agitated, making a loud churring noise. I finally investigated to find that the chick was dead. In retrospect only one parent was seen at a time at the nest, even soon after hatching. Usually one parent keeps the chicks warm while the other brings food. I can only assume that it had been a one-parent family. However I cannot understand why they did not survive when the numbers dropped to three and the chicks could be left on their own for a little while. Perhaps the young were poisoned by food contaminated as a result of spraying with insecticide somewhere outside the garden.

The Blackbird with five young continued to prosper until one evening a fledged youngster sat on a twig near the nest. I hoped that by the morning the rest would have left the nest. However the following morning a dead young Blackbird lay on the lawn near the nest. It had no sign of injury. I investigated and found one dead nestling still in the nest. What had happened? Had one or both parents been killed? Had the fledgling left the nest prematurely as the brood was left starving? I do not know. It is very disheartening but to coin a phrase it is nature's way and that is why some birds produce so many young.

The whole clutch of five Great Tit eggs failed to hatch. They had been laid in an end-compartment of a terrace box and were incubated for a week longer than the normal two weeks. Only the hen bird incubates. Eventually she gave up and the nest was abandoned. On investigation I found that the eggs were infertile. The strange thing is that last year a Great Tit nested in the same compartment in the same box. When the eggs had not hatched after four weeks I took pity on the mother and removed them. They too were infertile. Was it a coincidence? Was it the same bird and does it always lay infertile eggs? Another mystery in the wildlife garden.

On a happier note, the six young Wrens have all survived and have fledged successfully, as have a brood of five Dunnocks from a nest in cotoneaster on the house wall. The two broods of Starlings have fledged and the garden is no longer filled with their raucous calls.

August *(1)*

This morning on looking out of the living room window I saw a male Sparrowhawk straddling a dead Chaffinch. It was only two metres away from the bird-table and had killed the bird as it visited the table. I curbed my immediate natural reaction of concern for the unfortunate finch and accepted that this was purely a normal and frequent event in the wild. The bird-table with its ensemble of feeders is naturally an attraction for the garden birds, as also the Sparrowhawk, but not for the same reason!

The bird-table has been a success this summer. The nyjer seed has at last attracted Goldfinches, up to five adults at a time, and on one occasion a brood of four young. These attractive little finches are distinguished from their parents by the absence of black, white and red patterns on their heads. I recently purchased a new nyjer feeder. It consists of a plastic tube with two tiny holes in the side large enough for only one tiny black seed to be removed at a time by the fine beak of a Goldfinch. In no time at all the Goldfinches found these holes and spent considerable periods of time feeding there, much to the frustration of others at the table. No other birds could feed on this dispenser, as their beaks are too thick.

One morning a neat brown bird, slightly less bulky than a House Sparrow, was seen feeding on sunflower kernels. Its chocolate-brown head with white cheeks and black markings identified this bird as a Tree Sparrow. This attractive little seed eater, which had become quite scarce, has increased in numbers recently, thanks to the provision of feeding areas at the edges of fields and suitably positioned nest-boxes in hedgerows. On some days I observed two feeding. One feeding characteristic I noticed was that one would pick up a sunflower kernel, fly down to a breeze block, peck pieces off it to make it smaller and fly off, always in the same direction with the reduced piece in its beak. I assume it was taking food to its nest.

An adult female Great Spotted Woodpecker, identified by the lack of crimson on its head and neck, was seen feeding a fledgling, identifiable by its crimson crown. A second youngster with a brighter crown was feeding itself. Perhaps the difference in the crown coloration of these young birds is due to a difference in gender.

For the last few weeks there has been a continuous noise from over a hundred Jackdaws, mostly young ones, which have set up their home in the high hedge. After a time the cacophony became as irritating as canned laughter on the television. They dispersed during the day to forage, only to return noisily to roost in the evening.

August *(2)*
Some weeks ago I saw a small brown shape slide out, as if on wheels, from the cover of a ferny bank onto the flagstones below the bird-table. It resembled a tiny guinea pig. It was of course a vole, scavenging amongst the seeds and husks that had fallen from the feeders. In two other areas of the garden I also noticed a vole darting out in full view to grab an unseen morsel and scuttle back to the cover of the flowerbed. Was this a single individual or several? Short of catching one and marking it I cannot be certain, but I think there were more than one. These cute little mammals, so unlike the pointed-nosed Long-tailed Field-mice, were likely to be Bank Voles. As their name implies, their refuges were a banked-up flowerbed and a rockery. They had longish tails. Their near-cousins, the Field Voles, have somewhat shorter tails. One vole got quite used to me and scuttled out onto the lawn, nearly to my feet, a tempting snack for any hovering Kestrel.

The wildlife pond has become matted with invasive New Zealand pigmyweed. I have previously suggested thinning out this weed, as it is a medium for spawning newts, but it can soon take over a pond. I resolved to remove this alien plant. What a job it was! We had to resort to using hedge-shears to chop through the near-solid vegetation. I now think it should be removed from a pond as soon as it is seen, before it can get a hold.

I cannot remember a year when there have so few colourful butterflies in the garden. The buddleia is heavy with nectar-laden flowers, yet until recently only white butterflies have been seen, with the occasional Peacock and Red Admiral. There was a visit from a Comma butterfly earlier in the summer and a Small Copper butterfly was recently seen nectaring on borage. This small active butterfly lays its eggs on sorrel. Its numbers have fallen in recent years so I was pleased to have a visit from this attractive little insect. Its copper colouring distinguishes it from any other extant British butterfly

Kestrel

On 11th August I was excited to see a small silvery-blue butterfly hovering round a holly bush in the garden. Its name, appropriately enough, is the Holly Blue, and it is only the second time I have observed one here. In the spring this patchily distributed butterfly lays its eggs on the flower buds of holly and until recently it was thought to have only one generation a year in north Cumbria. In the south of England the Holly Blue has a second generation when eggs are usually laid on the flower buds of ivy. Over the last few years sightings of this insect have been made in late summer, indicating that a second generation must occur here too. There is an abundance of ivy in the garden so some eggs of this pretty little butterfly may be laid on the ivy flower buds.

September

Our dismal summer is sliding soggily into autumn. We have not had two consecutive dry days and the garden is waterlogged. I planted some bulbs recently and found that the soil was wet and clingy, the first time for years I have found it so. In spite of the rain the paucity of butterflies has been redressed recently. A minute of sunshine initiates a burst of Peacock and Red Admiral butterflies on the buddleia.

Before the end of August the approach of autumn is heralded by the plaintive thin winter song of the Robin. It had no competition from most of the other garden songbirds, now silent. It is now some weeks since I caught a glimpse out of the corner of my eye of a fleeting shape scurrying across the living room at dusk. The arrival of these house spiders at the end of summer can cause considerable distress to any arachnophobe in the household. It is said that these are males looking for females and as the females are bigger, one can be thankful that females do not chase males.

The moth-trap also has indicator species. When I capture the first Canary-shouldered Thorn of the year I feel slightly depressed, as it is the first sign of the end of summer. This is followed by several species of Sallow moths, predominantly yellow in colour as if reflecting the change in colour of the vegetation on which they are found. Later will be the Autumnal and November Moths, dismal dull-grey insects, nearly identical in appearance and which can only be identified from each other by examining their private parts.

October

We are now entering what I think of as being the dead period of the year. The plants have stopped growing and most of the birds have stopped singing. The summer migrants have left and as yet the autumn migrants have not arrived. The wildlife gardener could easily sink into a state of torpor and indolence if he did not take stock and think of preparing for the new season ahead. It is again time to check all the nest-boxes, making certain they have been cleaned out of any old nesting material. If a box has not been occupied for several years it could be repositioned, avoiding direct sunshine and prevailing wind and rain.

The ivy is now in flower, attracting several species of moth. The flowers of Michaelmas daisy and sedum are providing nectar for a few late butterflies, particularly Red Admirals. This should make us think about planting other butterfly-friendly plants to attract not only the adults but also to provide food for their caterpillars. Two suitable native plants that provide food for Green-veined Whites and Orange-tip caterpillar, are lady's-smock or cuckooflower and garlic mustard. Encourage sorrel for Small Coppers. Members of the cabbage family and nasturtiums provide food for Small and Large White butterflies. Nettles are the larval food plant of Red Admirals, Small Tortoiseshells, Peacocks and Commas. Unfortunately they have to grow in an open sunny position, not usually a welcome scenario for the fastidious gardener. Happily there are plenty of nettles around without feeling you have to have them in the garden.

The only excitement to break the gentle slow decay of autumn was the arrival of a Southern Hawker Dragonfly at the ponds. It was seen hawking for insects, hence its name. It interspersed its fantastic aerobatic displays with pit stops on the mossy stones surrounding the pond. It was probing with the end of its abdomen as if searching for a suitable medium in which to lay its eggs.

We will soon be entering the dark time of the year with the interminable winter months ahead. With that gloomy prospect sometimes one wishes one was like a dormouse, hibernating for seven months of the year and waking up in the merry month of May. Meanwhile as compensation we can enjoy the glorious autumnal leaf colour.

November
The time of year that is the epitome of damp dreariness is here, November, but a few colourful autumn leaves remain. The horse-chestnut is one of the first trees to change colour in early autumn yet it retains most of its yellow leaves. The oak, one of the latest trees to burst into leaf in spring, can retain its leaves well into December. The annual bind of sweeping up the leaves is taking place. I place the soggy mass into large black polythene bags, perforate them with several holes and store them in a hidden corner for the leaves to rot down. They can be spread on the garden in a year's time.

Many more Goldfinches have made use of the bird table this year, to eat nyjer seed and sunflower kernels. I have adapted the nyjer seed-dispenser by drilling slightly larger holes, making it easier for the tiny seeds to be extracted. Two further feeding holes were drilled at right angles and a length of narrow dowelling attached making two more perches. The slightly larger holes make it possible for Coal Tits to access the food, causing a change of habit for this tiny tit. When Coal Tits feed at a peanut-feeder, they grab a nut and fly off with it to return a minute or two later to pick up another peanut. Because the nyjer seeds are so tiny the Coal Tits stay feeding for some time. Now that the birds are feeding at the table again the Bank Vole has returned and is taking advantage of the tiny pieces of nut falling from the table.

Some years ago when walking through Newborough Forest on Anglesey I was surprised firstly to hear and then to see large numbers of Ravens. These birds, the largest of our corvids, were unattached youngsters assembling to court and find mates. They had come from many miles around. A similar phenomenon has arisen in my garden where over the last few weeks large numbers of Jackdaws, smaller members of the Corvid family, have been assembling and performing aerial acrobatics, wheeling and diving, and calling all the time. I wonder if this, like the Raven assembly, is to do with finding a mate for the coming season.

December
November ended and December began with a period of hard frosts. This has caused an influx of birds into the garden to feed at the bird table. As I was moving the table to clean around it, and even while still clutching the pedestal, something enchanting happened. A flock of about a dozen fairy-like apparitions arrived, six of them landing on the tit-feeder which hung only a foot from my chest. I froze and there they stayed for some minutes, pecking at the peanuts and flitting around like butterflies, making quiet zipping noises. They were Long-tailed Tits. If only I had had my camera to hand to catch this magical moment!

Recently I have been watching one, and sometimes two, tiny restless birds flitting lightly around the tips of evergreens looking for microscopic prey. These minute insectivorous birds are Goldcrests, distinguished as their name suggests by their narrow golden crowns. I am always amazed how such fragile creatures can survive everything the winter weather throws at them.

Another visit was not as enchanting but equally interesting. The ponds had been covered with netting to catch fallen leaves. When they were ice-free I scattered floating fish pellets on the surface. Over a period of days they disappeared and I thought the fish were eating them. Then at first light one morning I saw a dapper long-tailed black-and-white bird walking on the netting at the edge of the ponds picking up and eating the pellets. The Magpie had found a new food-source. Shortly I will remove the netting, as fallen leaves are no longer a problem. This opportunist will then have to learn to walk on water.

In the garden shed I had a pair of rubber gardening-gloves with cloth lining. I recently found that all the fingers of both gloves had been chewed. The rubber had gone and pieces of the fabric were left scattered about. I do not know if a mouse gets any nutritional value from rubber but if it does not, why does it chew it? Does it like the flavour?

Now is the time of year when we have invasions of Redwings and Fieldfares from northern Europe. As yet these thrushes have not visited the garden but when they do they will find a plentiful supply of windfall apples left for them on the ground. Other even more welcome winter visitors are Waxwings, which arrive in occasional irruptions from Scandinavia. These attractive Starling-sized migrants have been seen locally. This year flocks of up to six hundred have been reported from all around the area. They descend on trees already claimed by local thrushes, which try to drive the invaders away from their food reserves. The invasion may have been caused by a failure of the northern European rowanberry crop, their favourite food, or there may have been an explosion in numbers after a particularly good rowan year. Whatever the cause these attractive birds are a welcome sight. They look like large plump finches with prominent crests and white, yellow and waxy red markings on their wings, hence their name.

Wonderful photographs of these colourful birds were e-mailed to me. How times have changed since I started writing this diary.

Postscript

Since beginning to write the column for the *Cumberland News* in 1994 subtle changes have been observed. The numbers and variety of garden birds have increased. For fifteen years I did not see a woodpecker in the garden but in the last few years there have been regular visits by Great Spotted Woodpeckers, often in a family group. There has been a considerable increase of Goldfinch numbers at the bird-table and there is almost a daily visit of family parties of Long-tailed Tits. This increase may in part explain the increasingly frequent visits of Sparrowhawks. Feeding habits of some birds are changing as they learn to cling to the feeders. Birds such as Dunnock and Robin are now regularly seen using the nut feeders when once that would have been unusual.

The diversity of insects, particularly butterflies and moths, has increased in the last few years. Up to ten years ago I had not seen a Comma butterfly in the garden but in the last few years I have had at least a half-dozen visits from this insect. It has now been found further north across the Scottish border. The Blair's Shoulder-knot moth has moved into the village after a rapid spread north from the Isle of Wight in a little over half a century, helped by the widespread planting of Leylandii cypress. I have caught several moths new to Cumberland, possibly because of climate change.

In July this year I was excited to see a Red Squirrel wrapped round the tit-feeder on the bird-table, a first for the garden. The near-complete absence of hedgehogs in the garden continues to be a cause for concern.

Garden Centres have become the new leisure-shopping venues, selling feeders, food and props of all kinds. It is now much easier to provide for wildlife in the garden. People have become much more aware of environmental issues, the word *green* taking on a whole new depth of meaning with positive implications for our gardens and farms.

The changes and events that I have observed, notebook to hand, have taken place in less than a generation in a modest garden. There are many unanswered questions. It is only by observation of change that problems can be spotted and hopefully put right so that all gardens are havens for wildlife.

Richard Little

Richard Little's early years were spent in what was then the East Riding of Yorkshire. He was born in Beverley in 1936 and from the age of 11 he lived in Bridlington. His earliest explorations of the large area of commonland, known as the 'Westwood', in Beverley, and the cliffs and countryside near Bridlington fostered in him a deep interest in creatures of the wild.

After National Service in Germany he started work in the chemical laboratories of The Distillers Company Ltd. in south London, working in his own time for further qualifications. Whilst in the southeast he met and married Liz, a nurse from Cumbria. Richard decided that the chemical industry was not for him and he trained as a teacher. He found a job back in Hull as a science teacher.

The call of the wild tempted Richard to seek employment in Zambia under the auspices of the Ministry of Overseas Development, teaching science but relishing the chance to get to know a different sort of natural environment. Had personal problems not intervened Richard, Liz and their two children might well have stayed in Africa, but Liz had to come back to England while Richard finished his contract. She came back to her home of North Cumbria and Richard was eventually to spend the rest of his working life in a school in Carlisle.

Richard now began to explore the wonderful environment of Cumbria and to develop further his interests by observing and recording, particularly birds, butterflies and moths. On the last-named group he became something of an authority. He also completed a remarkable long-term project to climb every summit of 2,000 feet or more in England, all meticulously recorded in a diary. His interest in recording the minutiae of wildlife activity in his own garden has led to this book, A Cumbrian Wildlife Garden, by way of a monthly column in the Cumberland News.

Richard Little died in September, 2009.

Christine Isherwood, illustrator

Based in south Cumbria, Christine is a well-established artist and illustrator working mainly on wildlife and landscape subjects. Much of her work in recent years has gone into book illustrations, meticulous drawings in pen-and-ink. She is at present engaged in illustrating a series of guide-books for walkers covering the whole of Scotland.